Teaching
Comprehension and Exploring Multiple Literacies

Strategies From The Reading Teacher

Timothy V. Rasinski

Nancy D. Padak

Brenda Weible Church

Gay Fawcett

Judith Hendershot

Justina M. Henry

Barbara G. Moss

Jacqueline K. Peck

Elizabeth (Betsy) Pryor

Kathleen A. Roskos

Editors

INTERNATIONAL
Reading
Association

800 Barksdale Road, PO Box 8139
Newark, Delaware 19714-8139, USA
www.reading.org

The International Reading Association attempts, through its publications, to provide a forum for a wide spectrum of opinions on reading. This policy permits divergent viewpoints without implying the endorsement of the Association.

Director of Publications   Joan M. Irwin
Editorial Director, Books and Special Projects   Matthew W. Baker
Special Projects Editor   Tori Mello Bachman
Permissions Editor   Janet S. Parrack
Associate Editor   Jeanine K. McGann
Production Editor   Shannon Benner
Editorial Assistant   Pamela McComas
Publications Coordinator   Beth Doughty
Production Department Manager   Iona Sauscermen
Art Director   Boni Nash
Senior Electronic Publishing Specialist   Anette Schütz-Ruff
Electronic Publishing Specialist   Cheryl J. Strum
Electronic Publishing Assistant   John W. Cain

Library of Congress Cataloging-in-Publication Data
Teaching comprehension and exploring multiple literacies : strategies from The reading teacher / Timothy Rasinski ... [et al.]..
    p.   cm.
  Includes bibliographical references.
  ISBN 0-87207-281-9
    1. Reading comprehension.   2. Reading (Elementary).   3. Education, Elementary—Activity programs.   I.Rasinski, Timothy V.   II. International Reading Association.   III. Reading teacher.
  LB1573.7.T43   2000
  372.41'6—dc21   00-058101

Contents

About the editors

Timothy V. Rasinski
Professor of Education
Kent State University
Kent, Ohio, USA

Nancy D. Padak
Professor, Education; Director, Reading
   & Writing Center
Kent State University
Kent, Ohio, USA

Brenda Weible Church
Principal of Seiberling Elementary
   School
Akron Public Schools
Akron, Ohio, USA

Gay Fawcett
Executive Director of the Research
   Center for Educational Technology
Kent State University
Kent, Ohio, USA

Judith Hendershot
Teacher
Field Local Schools
Mogadore, Ohio, USA

Justina M. Henry
Literacy Collaborative-Project Trainer
The Ohio State University
Columbus, Ohio, USA

Barbara G. Moss
Research Associate
CASAS
San Diego, California, USA

Jacqueline K. Peck
PT3 Project Director
Kent State University
Kent, Ohio, USA

Elizabeth (Betsy) Pryor
Educational consultant; retired as super-
   visor of K-12 Reading/Language Arts
   for Columbus Public Schools
Worthington, Ohio, USA

Kathleen A. Roskos
Professor
John Carroll University
University Heights, Ohio, USA

Introduction

Make no mistake, comprehension is what reading is all about: Reading is comprehension. Reading has been described as the "process of constructing meaning from written texts...a holistic act" that depends on "the background of the reader, the purpose for reading, and the context in which reading occurs" (Anderson, Hiebert, Scott, & Wilkinson, 1985, p. 7). It is more than simply adding the meaning of the words (Harris & Hodges, 1995). Whether reading a story, directions for putting together a household appliance, a number in a telephone directory, or a piece of poetry, comprehension is the primary goal.

As teachers of literacy, then, we must have as an instructional goal, regardless of age, grade, or achievement level, the development of students as purposeful, engaged, and ultimately independent comprehenders. There is no way around it. No matter what grade level you teach, no matter what content you teach, no matter what texts you teach with, your goal is to improve students' comprehension and understanding.

But, comprehension is a complex process. Each individual comprehends differently because each comes to the reading task with different backgrounds, experiences, and abilities. No two readers construct the same meaning from a text, and no reader constructs exactly the same meaning as the author intended (Goodman, 1996). In addition, as children progress in their reading development, comprehension becomes increasingly sophisticated. As they mature, readers need to become increasingly strategic in their ability to construct meaning from text.

Comprehension involves what the reader knows as well as the nature of the text itself. It involves the type of text to be read—narrative, expository, poetry, etc. It involves the purpose for reading. And, it requires a variety of strategies to be shared with students. Depending on the nature and type of text to be read, the purpose for the reading, and the background knowledge of the reader, the instructional strategy employed by the teacher may differ. The more engaging and transparent approaches to comprehension that a teacher has at his or her disposal, the more successful that teacher will be in moving students toward thorough understanding of the texts they read.

With this collection of articles, we hope to add to your cache of comprehension instruction strategies with these classroom-tested ideas and approaches. Numerous strategies for helping students comprehend different types of texts and different forms of literacy are provided in this book. Activities for teaching young children about the features of narrative such as character, setting, problem, and solution are included along with strategies designed to support children as they create their own narrative texts. Other activities focus on comprehending expository texts found in content materials. A number of interesting variations and extensions of the K-W-L strategy are featured, as are ideas for using anticipation guides and graphic organizers.

This book also explores the notion of different forms of literacy. From technology-related literacy to visual literacy to theater literacy to music literacy, understanding of these forms of representation also is key to successful school experiences and an enriched and fulfilling life.

The articles in this volume have been drawn primarily from the Teaching Reading department of *The Reading Teacher* during our 6-year tenure as *RT* editors. This section of the journal is devoted to practical instructional strategies for classrooms, reading clinics, and homes. The ideas and support materials included in this themed anthology are examples of authentic and thoughtful classroom practice. The educators who have contributed to this volume subscribe to a broad understanding of the importance of literacy learning: That literacy is central to all learning and that literacy is learned through the work of dedicated and caring teachers at every grade level. The purpose of this book, then, is to present to our audience teacher-tested ideas, resources, and activities to make comprehension instruction in all forms of literacy more effective and engaging for students.

The articles in this volume were submitted by teachers from around the world as examples of best and innovative practice in their own classrooms. During our tenure, we received thousands of articles of this type. Only a select few of these articles were actually chosen for publication in *The Reading Teacher*. Each article went through a review process that consisted of at least three separate readings and rankings. Only those that were given the highest ratings were actually published. For this present volume, we examined again those articles that appeared in *RT*. Again we read and rated them, primarily for clarity, purpose, adherence to a particular theme, ease of implementation, and adaptability in a variety of classroom and other educational settings. Only those articles that met these high standards and criteria were chosen for this volume. So, with this volume, you are reading the very best of the best of practical comprehension strategies from *The Reading Teacher*.

The ideas and strategies offered in this volume will improve your ability to help students make sense of what they read. We hope you will adopt many of these approaches that have been demonstrated effective through the proving ground of real classroom instruction.

We have enjoyed our collaboration with the authors of these articles, and we have come to appreciate the tireless work of dedicated and selfless reading teachers around the world. We hope that you, teachers and teacher educators, will find the ideas and resources in this book helpful, supportive, and energizing as we all work toward a fully literate global society.

TR, NP, JH, BM,
BC, GF, TH,
JP, BP, KR

REFERENCES

Anderson, R.C., Hiebert, E., Scott, J., & Wilkinson, I. (1985). *Becoming a nation of readers.* Washington, DC: U.S. Department of Education.

Goodman, K. (1996). *On reading.* Portsmouth, NH: Heinemann.

Harris, T.L., & Hodges, R.E. (1995). *The literacy dictionary: The vocabulary of reading and writing.* Newark, DE: International Reading Association.

Story development using wordless picture books

Colleen Reese

Volume 50, Number 2, October 1996

In the summer of 1992, I applied for a grant to buy 44 wordless picture books (36 different titles) for my second-grade students. Their assignment was to write descriptive sentences to accompany the pictures. The objectives were for students to develop a sense of story, to use higher level thinking skills, and to develop their writing skills. The book *Wordless/Almost Wordless Picture Books* (Richey & Puckett, 1992) was a good resource for listing books that matched my criteria: The books could have no written text to accompany the pictures and had to be available in print.

Eight of the wordless picture books were read together as a class. Twelve of the books were used with pair/share partners and 24 were used by individuals. Through discussion and critical examination of the details of the illustrations, students wrote sentences that effectively complemented the pictures. The project was evaluated when the books were shared with other classrooms by peer feedback to such questions as "Did the words go with the pictures?" and "Did the story make sense?"

Whole class

The first wordless picture book for which my class wrote the text was an alphabet book entitled *Animal Alphabet* (Kitchen, 1984). The objective was to have the children describe each picture by writing a sentence. After the description of the picture was agreed upon by the class, I wrote the sentence on paper and immediately affixed it to the accompanying page.

After the book was completed, each child read a page orally. Two children were then picked to read the book to the principal, and two other children read the book to a first-grade classroom.

As an evaluation, the first graders were asked if they thought the story made sense. The two second-grade readers shared the first-grade responses with their classmates upon their return to class. The class then decided if revisions needed to be made.

Encouraged by a positive response, my second graders eagerly awaited the next wordless picture book, *How Santa Claus Had a Long and Difficult Journey Delivering His Presents* (Krahn, 1970). On the day the book was introduced, we discussed what was happening in the pictures. On the second day, the children dictated sentences that went with the pictures. The sentences were short and often used different tenses: "Two angels come along and Santa gets an idea. They turned the sled over and lifted Santa back into the sleigh." Two different children visited another first-grade classroom to read the completed product and returned with positive evaluative comments.

After the children worked through 8 wordless picture books together, their writing improved, and they became increasingly willing to revise. Their sentences were longer and more descriptive and used conversation. For instance "Mother talked to little mouse" became, "'What are you doing here?' asked Mother."

The final book my class did together was *Flying Jake* (Smith, 1988). For this book, the children decided to write the story in the first person. They used good connecting words such as *next*, *then*, and *but* so that not all of the sentences would start the same way. Word balloons were utilized to show the thoughts of various characters on a page. For example, "You dirty rat!" and "Oh my golly gee!" were two exclamations used in word balloons to show the characters were upset with the bird. We shared this book with a fourth-grade classroom.

Partners

By this time my students were anxious to do something on their own. I paired the children by putting a skilled reader and speller with a less skilled reader and speller.

First everyone made a list of things to remember while writing: Use capitals and periods, don't start all the sentences the same way, use linking words, try to use the same tense throughout the story, when using conversation remember quotation marks, give the characters names, and writing in the first person is permitted. (Such a list of ideas could never have been formulated had it not been for the class modeling that was done previously. Such modeling became the source of important tools for expressing ideas and learning strategies that could be used by my students to complete stories with a partner and on their own.)

I gave a wordless picture book to each pair/share team. The partners looked at the pictures and discussed what sentences could go with the pictures. The next day, each pair/share partner received a packet of self-sticking notes to use when writing their sentences. Both partners read the finished product to each other, checking to see if the story made sense and making corrections where needed.

Each pair/share team gave its book to me for typing. Many partners gave very specific instructions as to how they wanted certain pages typed (e.g., using all capitals to show excitement, using speech balloons above characters, and using an ellipsis to lead to the next page). Finally, the partners picked a class that would enjoy hearing them share their story.

Individuals

The time finally came for the children to choose from 24 titles a wordless picture book to complete independently. Individually they did everything the class had done as a group: (a) looked at the entire book and thought about the story; (b) used self-sticking notes to combine the story with the pictures; (c) reread their story, checking for readability, correct grammar, and punctuation; and (d) handed in the completed book along with any directions.

Later, students read each completed book to the class. Then, one by one, kindergarten, first, and second grades were invited to the cafeteria to listen to the completed books. Each visitor sat with one of the authors who, after reading the story, asked the questions: (a) Did the sentences match the pictures? (b) Did you like the story? (c) What was your favorite part and why? and (d) What was your favorite illustration and why? The answers to these questions gave each child personal feedback on whether they had managed to effectively write a story to go with the pictures. After listening to one story, the visitors rotated and listened to another story.

Evaluation and summary

The project entered the final stage when each child took his or her complet-

Wordless picture books used in the project

Bang, M. (1980). *The grey lady and the strawberry snatcher*. New York: Four Winds.

Bonners, S. (1989). *Just in passing*. New York: Lothrop, Lee & Shepard.

Brown, C. (1989). *The patchwork farmer*. New York: Greenwillow.

Cristini, E., & Puricelli, L. (1984). *In the pond*. New York: Picture Book Studio, Simon & Schuster.

Day, A. (1985). *Good dog, Carl*. New York: Simon & Schuster.

Day, A. (1989). *Paddy's pay-day*. New York: Viking Kestrel.

Drescher, H. (1987). *The yellow umbrella*. New York: Bradbury.

Goodall, J.S. (1977). *The surprise picnic*. New York: Margaret K. McElderry.

Goodall, J.S. (1984). *Paddy under water*. New York: Margaret K. McElderry.

Hutchins, P. (1971). *Changes*. New York: Macmillan.

Kitchen, B. (1984). *Animal alphabet*. New York: Dial.

Krahn, F. (1970). *How Santa Claus had a long and difficult journey delivering his presents*. New York: Dell.

Krahn, F. (1985). *Amanda and the mysterious carpet*. New York: Clarion.

McCully, E.A. (1984). *Picnic*. New York: HarperCollins.

McCully, E.A. (1985). *First snow*. New York: HarperCollins.

McCully, E.A. (1987). *School*. New York: Harper & Row.

MacGregor, M. (1988). *On top*. New York: Morrow.

Mayer, M. (1967). *A boy, a dog and a frog*. New York: Dial.

Mayer, M. (1969). *Frog, where are you?* New York: Dial.

Mayer, M. (1973). *Frog on his own*. New York: Dial.

(continued)

Wordless picture books used in the project (continued)

Mayer, M. (1974). *Frog goes to dinner.* New York: Dial.

Mayer, M., & Mayer, M. (1971). *A boy, a dog, a frog and a friend.* New York: Dial.

Mayer, M., & Mayer, M. (1975). *One frog too many.* New York: Dial.

Ormerod, J. (1981). *Sunshine.* New York: Lothrop, Lee & Shepard.

Ormerod, J. (1982). *Moonlight.* New York: Lothrop, Lee & Shepard.

Prater, J. (1985). *The gift.* New York: Viking Kestrel.

Schories, P. (1991). *Mouse around.* New York: Farrar, Straus & Giroux.

Smith, L. (1988). *Flying Jake.* New York: Macmillan.

Spier, P. (1982). *Rain.* New York: Delacorte.

Spier, P. (1986). *Dreams.* New York: Doubleday.

Tafuri, N. (1983). *Early morning in the barn.* New York: Greenwillow.

Tafuri, N. (1985). *Rabbit's morning.* New York: Greenwillow.

Tafuri, N. (1988). *Junglewalk.* New York: Greenwillow.

Tafuri, N. (1990). *Follow me!* New York: Greenwillow.

Turkle, B. (1976). *Deep in the forest.* New York: E.P. Dutton.

Young, E. (1984). *The other bone.* New York: HarperCollins.

ed book home to share with his or her family.

Throughout the 6 months of the grant project my students learned to write stories in complete sentences, to expand their ideas to better describe the pictures, and to produce a meaningful story. They learned to summarize pages with multiple pictures, at the same time making sure the sentences matched the action shown in the pictures. Linking words were used to make the story cohesive, and sentences were begun in different ways. Students learned to use quotation marks for conversations, commas for items in a series, exclamation marks for emphasis, ellipses to tell the reader that the thought was not yet complete, and correct verb tenses. Many children personalized their stories by giving names to the characters and places. Thus, the children were able to build their reading and writing skills and strategies to ultimately produce a unique book.

REFERENCE

Richey, V., & Puckett, K. (1992). *Wordless/almost wordless picture books.* Englewood, CO: Libraries Unlimited.

Book character cards

Kathy Morrow

VOLUME 49, NUMBER 7, APRIL 1996

Looking for an alternative to the traditional book report? Creating book character cards is one way my students share books. Most children enjoy collecting all kinds of trading cards, from cards of famous sports figures to comic book characters. Students choose a central character from their current reading workshop book or any book they have previously read and apply the trading card format to a presentation of that character. The book character cards activity promotes reading, writing, and sharing by using a medium children are familiar with and interested in.

For my classes, this activity usually follows minilessons on character types and analysis. To introduce book character cards and create interest, I share my collection of race-car-driver cards with the class. Students are then invited to bring their cards. (Caution: One-of-a-kind, valuable cards should not be brought to school.)

During the next class period, students show and talk about their cards in small groups. Through whole group discussion, students identify and classify the information on the commercial cards. Categories such as name, biographical data, statistics, and special awards are listed on the chalkboard or overhead transparency to help students decide what information to include on their book character cards.

Using index cards (ruled one side only) students create a card for the character from the book selected. The ruled side of the index card should list the book title, author, and character's name. (If the card is to be used as a quick check for comprehension of character types, that information should also be given. For example, protagonist-round-dynamic or antagonist-round-static.) Any special achievements and/or unusual, interesting facts about the character are listed.

The unruled side of the card is used for art work to depict the character. Students may draw, paste magazine pictures or photographs, or use computer graphics. They write their names or initials on this side to identify their work.

As students complete their book character cards, they again share, either in small groups or with the whole class. Afterwards, the finished cards can be kept in a small file box or can be bound using a single-hole punch and a metal ring. The collection is then placed in the room for easy access by students. Class collections may be done from year to year.

Book character cards are fun to make and provide information students can use when choosing books for self-paced reading. The cards can be used as a form of assessment regarding character types if the teacher desires. Readers may want to add cards to the collection throughout the year.

Find the features and connect them

Janet C. Richards
Joan P. Gipe
Mary Ann Necaise

VOLUME 48, NUMBER 2, OCTOBER 1994

Some children have limited knowledge of children's literature and little awareness about the parts of stories. They can usually name story characters, but they have difficulty recognizing other basic story features and their connections (e.g., settings, problems, solutions). We know that effective readers use this knowledge to guide their understanding and recall of narrative text (Fitzgerald & Teasley, 1986; Mandler & Johnson, 1977), so we want to help our students develop it. We created a game that provides opportunities for our students to share their thoughts about the key features of stories and their interconnections while also emphasizing story content (Fitzgerald, 1989).

Following a short teacher-led discussion about basic story features and their connections, a group of 6 to 8 players each receives a color-coded card from one of four story feature card stacks: characters, settings, problems, and solutions from a familiar story. The Figure shows examples of such cards for Jon Scieszka's *The True Story of the Three Little Pigs.*

Players take turns discarding and drawing cards from one of the four stacks until they can connect two story features (e.g., a problem and a solution, a character and a setting, a character and a problem). When connections are made, players display their two cards and share their thinking regarding the match. For example, a second grader in our program connected the card saying *Alexander T. Wolf* with the card *A house of straw.* She explained, "In *The True Story of the Three Little Pigs*, Alexander T. Wolf is a story character. The first little pig's house of straw is a setting. They connect because Alexander T. Wolf went to the straw house to get some sugar."

The next player connected *The wolf ran out of sugar* with *He went to the pig's house.* He said, "One of the problems in the story is that Alexander T. Wolf wanted to make a cake and he ran out of sugar. So he decided to get some sugar

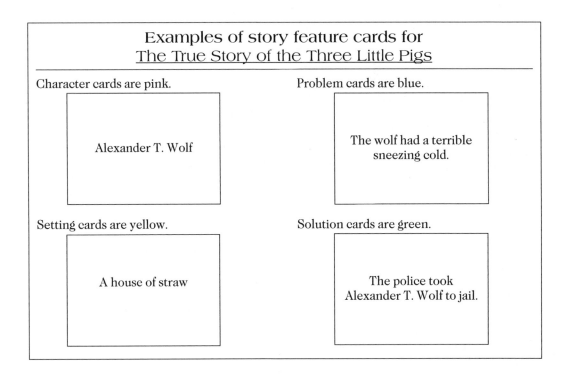

Examples of story feature cards for
The True Story of the Three Little Pigs

Character cards are pink.

Alexander T. Wolf

Problem cards are blue.

The wolf had a terrible sneezing cold.

Setting cards are yellow.

A house of straw

Solution cards are green.

The police took Alexander T. Wolf to jail.

from his neighbors, the pigs." He then added spontaneously, "But then the pigs started to have problems."

The game continues until players connect all of the story feature cards or until they cannot link any of the remaining cards.

When our students are familiar with the four basic features in stories, we encourage them to explore other aspects of story feature connections. For example, Alexander T. Wolf is a story character. At the same time, his actions are a big problem for the three little pigs. Similarly, the straw house is a story setting that becomes a problem for the first little pig when Alexander T. Wolf sneezes and blows it down on top of the pig. Thus, to expand the game further, we introduce other important story parts and their connections (e.g., the initiating event, connections within and across multiple story episodes, the final outcome or resolution).

Students also use blank cards to record their ideas about story features and their connections prior to writing their own stories.

Finding the story features and connecting them can be used with nonreaders as well. They listen to a story read or told by the teacher and then choose and connect pictures that illustrate the connections between the story's characters, settings, problems, and solutions. For example, after listening to *Goldilocks and the Three Bears* (Cauley, 1981), one child chose pictures of the three bears and Goldilocks to represent the characters and a picture of the forest to represent the setting. She explained, "Goldilocks went for a walk in the forest and the three bears lived in the forest." Another chose pictures of the three bowls of porridge as a problem and a picture of the three bears walking in the woods as a solution. She said, "The porridge was too hot, so the bears went for a walk in the woods to wait for the porridge to get cool."

Our students enjoy playing literacy games cooperatively. So, rather than awarding points to winning players, we encourage them to collaborate and share their thoughts with each other. Books are always available so that players can verify a story feature or feature match.

Observing our students as they play the game helps us to document growth in their understanding about the parts of stories and their interrelatedness. We also gain insights about children's verbal abilities, their willingness to take turns and follow the rules of a game, and their abilities to collaborate with peers (Castle, 1990; Surbeck & Glover, 1992).

REFERENCES

Castle, K. (1990). Children's invented games. *Childhood Education, 67,* 82–85.

Fitzgerald, J. (1989). Research on stories: Implications for teachers. In K. Muth (Ed.), *Children's comprehension of text* (pp. 2–36). Newark, DE: International Reading Association.

Fitzgerald, J., & Teasley, A. (1986). Effects of instruction in narrative structure on children's writing. *Journal of Educational Psychology, 78,* 424–433.

Mandler, J., & Johnson, N. (1977). Remembrance of things parsed: Story structure and recall. *Cognitive Psychology, 9,* 111–151.

Surbeck, E., & Glover, M. (1992). Seal revenge: Ecology games invented by children. *Childhood Education, 68,* 275–281.

CHILDREN'S BOOKS CITED

Cauley, L. (1981). *Goldilocks and the three bears.* New York: Putnam.

Scieszka, J. (1989). *The true story of the three little pigs.* New York: Viking.

Using games to help young and at-risk children respond to story characters

Janet C. Richards

Volume 47, Number 2, October 1993

As supervisors of an urban K–3 literature-based reading program, we note that young and at-risk children become more interested and involved in reading and listening to stories when we provide opportunities for them to respond personally to story characters. One approach we find effective is to create games that encourage children to share their opinions and thoughts about story characters, using information in stories to substantiate and support their ideas. The children in our program particularly enjoy the following games.

"Provide Evidence"

In the game "Provide Evidence," 6 to 8 players share their opinions about familiar story characters' personality attributes and behaviors. Each player receives six cards. Three cards come from a descriptive adjective deck and should include words such as *sad, happy, shrewd, wise, thoughtful, angry, scared, frightened,* *crafty, mean, wild, quiet, adventurous, mischievous, intelligent, foolish, rude, disobedient, fair, greedy,* etc. The other three cards come from a deck containing the names of story characters (e.g., Peter Rabbit, Al in Yorinks's *Hey, Al* [1986] or Margaret in Rabe's *The Balancing Girl* [1981]). Players take turns discarding and drawing a card from an adjective or character card stack until they can link an adjective with a story character. Once a match is made, they display the two cards, share their opinions regarding the match, and provide evidence from a story to support and explain their thinking.

For example, a third grader in our program linked the adjective

mean

with the character

Mr. McGregor

She explained, "Mr. McGregor in *The Tale of Peter Rabbit* was mean because he

---

13

chased Peter all around the garden." A first grader matched the adjective

> kind

with the character

> Mama Bear

saying, "Mama Bear in *Goldilocks and the Three Bears* was kind because she made porridge for her family." The game continues until players match all adjectives and character cards or until they cannot link any of the remaining cards.

"What Would Your Character Do?"

The game "What Would Your Character Do?" elicits 6 to 8 players' opinions regarding how story characters might think and act in contexts other than their original literary domains. Each player chooses a card containing the name of a familiar story character. Next, players listen to a scenario selected from a scenario card stack, such as:

> It was a dark and rainy night. Five friends and your character were watching television. At midnight everyone wanted to eat pizza. What would your character do?

Players then take turns explaining how their characters might respond in the situation described, supporting their reasoning by citing evidence stated in their character's original literary setting.

For example, a second grader in our program whose character was

> Little Red Hen

responded to the pizza scenario by saying, "My character, Little Red Hen, would go buy the pizza all by herself. In the story of *The Little Red Hen*, she always had to do everything herself." Another student said, "My character is

> Baby Bear

He wouldn't go out alone at night to get pizza. He's a baby and in the story of *Goldilocks and the Three Bears* he was always with his mom and dad."

Other scenarios appropriate for "What Would Your Character Do?" might include

1. You and your character encounter an alien from outer space. The alien, named ET, invites the two of you to tour his spaceship. He also wants you and your character to visit his planet. What questions would you and your character ask ET? What would you do? What would your character do?

2. Your character is left—home alone!!! The rest of the family has gone off on a 3-day vacation trip. Your character was left behind by mistake. What would your character do?

3. Your character forgets his/her homework. Has your character ever forgotten to bring homework to school be-

fore? Children who forget their home-work are required to stay after school. Your character has been invited to a birth-day party after school. What would your character do?

4. You and your character find a wallet on the ground. You look inside the wallet and discover a large amount of money. You and your character can't figure out who owns the wallet because there is no identification card. What would you do? What would your character do?

5. Your character is transported to a foreign land for 2 weeks. No one speaks your character's language, English. It is the only language your character speaks, reads, and writes. Your character needs food, a place to sleep, and money. What would your character do?

6. You and your character meet the President of the United States. You are each allowed to ask the President three questions. What three questions would you ask? Why? What three questions would your character ask? Why?

7. Your character is in second grade and cannot read or write. How would you help your character learn to read and write? How can the teacher help your character learn to read and write? What should your character do?

8. Your character grows up and be-comes a third-grade teacher. What type of teacher is your character? What does your character believe about third graders? What does your character need to know about third graders? Does your character work very hard as a teacher? Which subjects does your character like to teach the most and why? Which subjects does your character like to teach the least and why?

9. You and your character get to go to three movies. Which movies would you choose and why? Which three movies would your character choose and why?

10. You and your character make a list of your favorite books. Which books do you choose? Why? Which books does your character choose? Why?

Management and assessment

We find that children enjoy playing these games cooperatively. Therefore, rather than awarding points to winning players or teams, we encourage children to help each other come to conclusions about story characters and stimulate one another's thinking. Dictionaries and children's literature are always available so that we can assist players in checking the definition of an adjective or verifying a description of a particular story character.

We have discovered that observing children as they play "Provide Evidence" and "What Would Your Character Do?" offers us an alternative way to document growth in their cognitive, verbal, and social abilities. We gain insights about how children learn to cooperate, reason, solve problems, follow rules, negotiate, and explain ideas to peers (Castle, 1990; Surbeck & Glover, 1992). Observing children as they play these games also helps us to ascertain growth in their oral language abilities and comprehension of factual and inferential information about story characters.

REFERENCES

Castle, K. (1990). Children's invented games. *Childhood Education, 67*, 82–85.

Surbeck, E., & Glover, M. (1992). Seal revenge: Ecology games invented by children. *Childhood Education, 68*, 275–281.

CHILDREN'S BOOKS CITED

Cauley, L. (1981). *Goldilocks and the three bears*. New York: G.P. Putnam's Sons.

Galdone, P. (1974). *The little red hen*. New York: McGraw-Hill.

Potter, B. (1902). *The tale of Peter Rabbit*. New York: Warne.

Rabe, B. (1981). *The balancing girl*. New York: B.P. Dutton.

Yorinks, A. (1986). *Hey, Al*. New York: Farrar, Strauss & Giroux.

Getting to know story characters: A strategy for young and at-risk readers

Janet C. Richards
Joan P. Gipe

VOLUME 47, NUMBER 1, SEPTEMBER 1993

Young and at-risk readers who are familiar with children's literature can usually identify characters in a story, but they often have difficulty recognizing how authors reveal information about characters. For example, authors portray story characters directly by telling or describing factual information about them. Authors also use more subtle and indirect methods that require readers to infer information from what a character does, says, or thinks (Norton, 1992). We have developed a strategy called "Getting to Know My Character" that is useful for helping young and at-risk readers recognize information about story characters in order to increase their reading comprehension.

To introduce the strategy, the teacher displays a "Getting to Know My Character" map and a story excerpt that portrays a character through description, actions, conversations, and thoughts. The teacher says, "Today we're going to learn a new strategy that will help us recognize how authors give us information about story characters. Good readers recognize and use information about story characters to help them understand characters' feelings and how characters will act in certain situations. Information about story characters also helps us understand the meaning of a story." Then the teacher reads the story excerpt aloud as the children follow along (see Figure 1).

Next the teacher says, "At the beginning of this story the author tells us some important facts about Margaret." Then the teacher helps the children recognize this descriptive information by highlighting the appropriate portion of the passage and explaining her own thinking (e.g., "As I read the first sentence I learned that Margaret was good at balancing"). She also asks questions that help the children recognize additional descriptive information about Margaret (e.g., "What did the author tell us about Margaret and her wheelchair?"). The teacher models how to complete the map by printing this information in the Facts category of the Getting to Know My Character map (see Figure 2). She then encourages the children to share their personal thoughts and opinions about Margaret (e.g., "Why do you think Margaret used a wheelchair?" and "Do you think Margaret has used crutches for a long time?").

Next the teacher says, "As we read further, we learned more important information about Margaret from her actions." The teacher highlights this portion of the passage and also helps the children summarize Margaret's actions (e.g., "Margaret

---

Figure 1
Passage: The Balancing Girl

Margaret was good at balancing. She could balance a book on her head and glide along in her wheelchair. She could even balance herself on her crutches. One day Margaret made a private corner in the classroom. She worked carefully all morning and made a beautiful domino castle. When Margaret came back to her classroom after lunch, she saw that her castle was knocked down. "I DIDN'T DO IT!" shouted Tommy. Margaret said, "Yes you did Tommy, and you better never knock down anything I balance again, or YOU'LL BE SORRY!" Then Margaret made a new castle. When she finished, six dominoes fell down. "Oh no!" she thought. But, then the dominoes stopped falling. "Thank goodness," Margaret said to herself.

From *The Balancing Girl* by Berniece Rabe. Copyright 1981 by Berniece Rabe. Used by permission of Dutton's Children's Books, a division of Penguin Books USA Inc.

---

made a private corner"). She also helps the children infer information from Margaret's actions by modeling her own inferential thinking (e.g., "The part of the story that says Margaret made a private corner makes me think that Margaret wanted to work alone, because when I don't want to be interrupted I find a private place"). Then the teacher asks questions that encourage the children to use clues from Margaret's actions along with their background knowledge to infer additional information (e.g., "What type of a person would be able to build a beautiful domino castle?"). The teacher prints all of this information in the Actions category of the Getting to Know My Character map. Once again she encourages the children to share their ideas and opinions about Margaret.

The teacher continues the lesson by helping the children recognize further information about Margaret from Margaret's conversation with Tommy and from Margaret's thoughts after she rebuilt the castle. The teacher again highlights the appropriate portions of the passage and explains her own inferential thinking (e.g., "I think that Margaret was brave to speak up to Tommy" and "I say 'Oh no' to myself just like Margaret when I am worried"). The teacher also asks questions that help the children infer information from Margaret's and Tommy's conversation and from Margaret's thoughts (e.g., "How do you think that Margaret knew that Tommy knocked down her castle?" and "What would you do if you thought that someone had deliberately hurt one of your projects?"). All of this information is printed in the Conversation and Thoughts

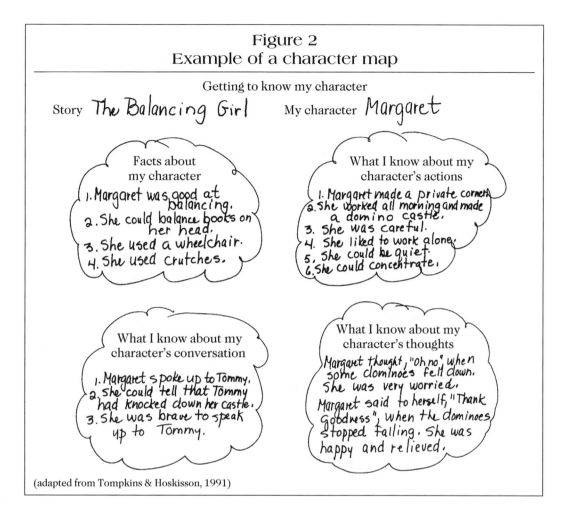

Figure 2
Example of a character map

Getting to know my character

Story **The Balancing Girl**   My character **Margaret**

> **Facts about my character**
> 1. Margaret was good at balancing.
> 2. She could balance books on her head.
> 3. She used a wheelchair.
> 4. She used crutches.

> **What I know about my character's actions**
> 1. Margaret made a private corner.
> 2. She worked all morning and made a domino castle.
> 3. She was careful.
> 4. She liked to work alone.
> 5. She could be quiet.
> 6. She could concentrate.

> **What I know about my character's conversation**
> 1. Margaret spoke up to Tommy.
> 2. She could tell that Tommy had knocked down her castle.
> 3. She was brave to speak up to Tommy.

> **What I know about my character's thoughts**
> Margaret thought, "oh no", when some dominoes fell down. She was very worried. Margaret said to herself, "Thank Goodness", when the dominoes stopped falling. She was happy and relieved.

(adapted from Tompkins & Hoskisson, 1991)

categories of the Getting to Know My Character map.

After a few similar lessons with appropriate story excerpts, young and at-risk readers usually are ready to read or listen to stories and complete their own Getting to Know My Character maps individually or with a partner. They can also use the maps to help recognize and compare and contrast information about multiple characters within or between stories (e.g., Goldilocks and Sleeping Beauty) and to plan how they will present story characters in their own creative writing.

REFERENCES

Norton, D. (1992). Engaging children in literature: Modeling inferencing of characterization. *The Reading Teacher, 46,* 64–67.

Tompkins, G., & Hoskisson, K. (1991). *Language arts content and teaching strategies* (2nd ed.). New York: Merrill.

KWLA: Linking the affective and cognitive domains

Thomas F. Mandeville

Volume 47, Number 8, May 1994

Learning does not occur in an affective vacuum. When readers consciously assign their own importance and interest to newly read information, they are likely to comprehend and remember that information better. Opportunities for including this affective dimension are readily available by extending the highly successful lesson format called Know, Wonder, Learn (KWL) (Ogle, 1986).

KWL is an instructional strategy based on a three column chart. Students brainstorm what they know about a topic in the first or Know column and generate questions they would like to have answered about that topic in the second or Wonder column. After reading, they use the third or Learn column to answer their questions and to list other new information they have learned. KWL Plus (Carr & Ogle, 1987) adds summarizing to the process.

To add an affective component to KWL or to KWL Plus, add a fourth column, Affect. Within that column, responses to several sets of affective domain questions are possible. To a question like "What do I find interesting?" in a lesson about insects, for example, some may reply, "The part I liked was that not all insects are harmful, some help people," or "I was interested in the fact that spiders are not insects because they have 8 legs, so now I want to find out what spiders are," or "It was interesting to learn that a caterpillar may become a butterfly someday—that's like the Ugly Duckling story."

Students may also reflect on the importance or value of the information by responding to questions such as "Why is this information important for me?" or "What will be different now?" or "How does it help me to know this information?" A student may write, "It is good to know that some people like to eat insects. Then I will not be shocked if I see someone eating a grasshopper or some ants." Another may write, "I know about the life cycle of a caterpillar-butterfly. Maybe this will help me understand the life cycle of other animals, especially other insects." Still another student may write, "Now I can tell a moth from a butterfly, because moths have fatter bodies and feathery antennae."

Finally, students may respond with new attitudes about their learning. For example, students may note that cicadas and other singing insects are held in great esteem by some Asian cultures. A student may write, "Next time I see an insect, I will not kill it until I know whether it will help me or harm me."

Discussion is an important feature of KWLA just as it is with KWL. When students talk about their affective responses and listen to the responses of others, their written responses will be of higher quality. Through discussion, students learn they have permission to have personal responses. Otherwise they may have some reluctance to risk venturing a feeling or identifying a value. Teachers may need to model interest statements and personal reactions to help establish a risk-free environment. At first some children may adopt the responses of the teacher or of another child, but as the students become more practiced at making affective responses within a safe environment, they will be more likely to recognize and share their own ideas.

Children strengthen the construction of their new knowledge when they expand their cognitive learning by recognizing their affective responses. By adding a fourth column to the KWL chart and expanding it to KWLA, students can assign their own relevance, interest, and personal value to their learning experiences.

REFERENCES

Carr, E., & Ogle, D. (1987). KWL Plus: A strategy for comprehension and summarization. *Journal of Reading, 30,* 626–631.

Ogle, D.M. (1986). K-W-L: A teaching model that develops active reading of expository text. *The Reading Teacher, 39,* 564–570.

Using paragraph frames to complete a K-W-L

Kathleen E. Weissman

VOLUME 50, NUMBER 3, NOVEMBER 1996

The K-W-L procedure (Ogle, 1986), "what I Know, what I Want to learn, and what I Learned," has been successful in helping me guide students to become independent learners. It enables them to identify not only what they already know, but what they want to know. I have modified the K-W-L strategy to help students realize that learning is continuous. Students need to take responsibility for their learning and actively pursue their own quest for knowledge (Ogle, 1986).

In my first-grade class, I often conclude the study of a topic with a "What we've learned" chart completed as a group. Students enjoy working together, and it is relatively easy to develop a brainstormed chart. I extended the L of K-W-L by adapting paragraph frames (Cudd & Roberts, 1989) to correspond with a particular topic and use them as another way to reach the L goal (see Figures 1 and 2). I provide a scaffold for students' thinking and writing by giving them sentence starters to help them with the task of writing about what they have learned. This modification provides both a way to assess the learning that has taken place on the topic and an opportunity for nonfiction writing.

Procedures for using paragraph frames to complete a K-W-L

After completing a unit, or when wanting to summarize a topic, I begin the "what we've Learned" by asking students to share verbally their ideas with the group. Next, I write an introductory sentence on a chart, and this allows the reader to know what the coming text will be about. Then I begin four or five sentences that need to be completed using the newly acquired information. We complete the sentences together. Many ideas are volunteered, and the class decides on the one that makes the most sense. Sometimes we combine more than one idea. I have found that complete modeling of this type of writing is necessary only two or three times.

Figure 1
Adapted paragraph frames to show what was learned

Brittany

I learned some new things about Frogs. For instance the

texisi frog makes a sound like a
dog. It also has enumys like
snakes foxs and peole. I think
wolvs and ciotys are also
enunys. Frogs are good beruse the
eat inses.

I also learned som peole eat frogs lage

Frogs are posonis.

However, the most interesting thing I learned was sring

peeper peep.

One question I still have is are all frogs

posonis?

Figure 2
Adapted paragraph frame to show what was learned

The life of a frog
Include a detailed illustration for each of these facts. Complete each unfinished sentence.

A female frog lays a clump of eggs in a pond. They are called frog-spawn.

The egg becomes _____

Soon the tadpole _____

Finally _____

This interactive writing provides the means to address several issues, including the use of transition words, spelling, syntax, and editing. Some students can contribute more than just the paragraph frame, while needier students feel successful when only completing the frame. In addition, the students not only are given possibilities for content area writing, but also are exposed to text structures found in expository writing that will help them in comprehension when reading independently (Cudd & Roberts, 1989).

As a final step, students include a detailed illustration with their completed paragraph frame. I have found that as students are encouraged to add details to their drawings, they are better able to understand the importance of including details to communicate ideas in writing (Cudd & Roberts, 1989).

The use of this technique has proven very effective with my students. I saw an almost immediate improvement in their nonfiction writing and a significant transfer of learning as the frames and language were used in other writing. In addition, it has also provided me with a meaningful way to assess their learning of a subject.

REFERENCES

Cudd, E., & Roberts, L. (1989). Using writing to enhance content area learning in the primary grades. *The Reading Teacher, 42,* 392–404.

Ogle, D. (1986). K-W-L: A teaching model that develops active reading of expository text. *The Reading Teacher, 39,* 564–570.

K-W-W-L: Questioning the known

Jan Bryan

VOLUME 51, NUMBER 7, APRIL 1998

The purpose of this article is to revisit and offer a suggestion to extend the K-W-L instructional activity (What I *Know*, What I *Want* to Learn, What I *Learned*) (Ogle, 1986). Since its earliest formal recognition, K-W-L has helped young learners develop appropriate questions for research and organize what they know. In recent years, K-W-L has been revised to address emerging educational needs. For example, in K-W-L Plus (Carr & Ogle, 1987), learners develop their own questions for study.

I have extended K-W-L in two ways. First, I scaffold for young learners so that they can generate questions from their knowledge. This encourages lifelong learning and guides students to continually refine what they know. Second, I extend K-W-L with the inclusion of a fourth column: the *where* column. I have found that young learners often generate wonderful questions but are then discouraged because they lack the resources to find their answers. When teachers include brainstorming sessions that focus on where specific information can be located, they facilitate young learners' research.

The following example is drawn from several planning sessions conducted with 9-year-olds in a rural school district in the midwestern U.S. I worked with this particular class as we planned a unit together to study connections between the midwest and the oceans. We began with a simple brainstorming session. I told the class that I was interested in learning about the oceans because I had heard that the quality of our lives is directly related to the quality of the oceans. I asked the children what they already knew about oceans. Because these are children from the midwest, I was not surprised to discover that they had developed only superficial concepts regarding oceans. Figure 1 lists the statements generated by this class.

Some problems of student-generated research are evident. First, how can a teacher build upon students' knowledge? Second, how can a teacher generate enthusiasm among children who seem to be in a state of equilibrium concerning their ocean knowledge? Third, how can teachers scaffold for children so that they can generate meaningful questions? Of course, these are powerful questions, and definitive answers are yet to be discov-

Figure 1
What the students knew about oceans

I know...	I want to learn...	Where I can learn this...	I have learned...
1. Oceans are salty.			
2. Salt water burns your eyes.			
3. Oceans have waves.			
4. There are more than 350 kinds of sharks.			
5. Hurricanes begin over oceans.			
6. Oceans have fish.			
7. Oceans have shells.			
8. The Beach Boys sing about oceans.			

ered. However, building upon knowledge by creating disequilibrium can facilitate meaningful discovery for young learners.

In K-W-W-L, disequilibrium is created when the teacher scaffolds for the students and questions the known. For example, the first known mentioned by the third-grade children was that oceans are salty. The challenge for the teacher is to pose all kinds of questions designed to question this known. I asked these students why oceans are salty while most lakes and rivers are not. I asked how much salt is in the water. I asked if all oceans contain the same amount of salt. After that, the students caught on and began to question the known. They finally decided to research the question of salt and why oceans are salty.

Next, I questioned the known concerning salt water burning eyes. I began with a simple question, "Has anyone ever tasted their own tears?" This is all the scaffold that was required before students began questioning the known. If our own tears are salty, then why does ocean salt ir-

ritate? This led to a second and third question, "Are there chemicals in the ocean?" and "Are these chemicals harming us?" Figure 2 lists the questions that the students generated as we questioned the known.

As the students questioned the known, their questions opened the avenue to more and more questions. In fact, one child commented, "This could go on forever!"

After questioning the known and generating new questions, the students and I brainstormed ideas for resources. Because we were far from any ocean, it was important that we explore varied avenues for discovery. This led to the second expansion of the original K-W-L strategy: the *where* column. As we looked at each question, I asked students to think of resources we could use, including people we could ask, to help us answer each question. Figure 3 lists their ideas.

What I found particularly intriguing about this brainstorming session was the number of times that the students re-

Figure 2
Student-generated questions

I know...	I want to learn...	Where I can learn this...	I have learned...
1. Oceans are salty.	1. Why are oceans salty?		
2. Salt water burns your eyes.	2a. Why does salt water burn? 2b. Are there chemicals in the ocean? 2c. Are these chemicals harmful?		
3. Oceans have waves.	3. What causes waves?		
4. There are more than 350 kinds of sharks.	4. Are all sharks dangerous?		
5. Hurricanes begin over oceans.	5. How can we be safe from hurricanes?		
6. Oceans have fish.	6. Are sea monsters, like the one in Loch Ness, real?		
7. Oceans have shells.	7. Why do shells make the sound of the ocean?		
8. The Beach Boys sing about oceans.	8. What are some surf songs?		

ferred to human resources for information. This leads to multiple opportunities to include authentic literacy experiences in the curriculum. These students now searched phone directories and made inquiries at universities and museums to locate the scientists, meteorologists, and marine biologists required to answer their questions. Then the students wrote appropriate letters asking these professionals to visit their class or to answer their questions in writing.

I was also intrigued by the experiments that the students began to design. As this session was closing, several children were busy outlining a waves experiment. They knew they wanted to test a wind theory, so they were designing ways to simulate wind across the ocean surface.

Students also made powerful connections between this K-W-W-L session and an earlier science experiment. Previously, students experimented with tuning forks by placing the forks in bowls of water to observe the action of sound waves. One

Figure 3
Student-generated resources

I know...	I want to learn...	Where I can learn this...	I have learned...
1. Oceans are salty.	1. Why are oceans salty?	• encyclopedia • ask a scientist • ask a marine biologist	
2. Salt water burns your eyes.	2a. Why does salt water burn?	• ask an optometrist	
	2b. Are there chemicals in the ocean?	• ask a scientist	
	2c. Are these chemicals harmful?	• ask a physician	
3. Oceans have waves.	3. What causes waves?	• go to the library • ask a marine biologist • ask a weather person • create an experiment	
4. There are more than 350 kinds of sharks.	4. Are all sharks dangerous?	• ask a marine biologist	
5. Hurricanes begin over oceans.	5. How can we be safe from hurricanes?	• ask a weather person	
6. Oceans have fish.	6. Are sea monsters, like the one in Loch Ness, real?	• surf the Internet	
7. Oceans have shells.	7. Why do shells make the sound of the ocean?	• ask a scientist • create an experiment	
8. The Beach Boys sing about oceans.	8. What are some surf songs?	• ask the music teacher	

student related this experiment to a question about sea shells and waves, noting that it was probably moving sound waves that sounded like the ocean.

As their research continues, these students will learn more about waves, sharks, the Beach Boys, and hurricanes. What excites me is not what they will learn, but that they will continue to question the known and think about ways to find new information.

REFERENCES

Carr, E., & Ogle, D. (1987). K-W-L plus: A strategy for comprehension and summarization. *Journal of Reading, 30,* 626–631.

Ogle, D. (1986). K-W-L: A teaching model that develops active reading of expository text. *The Reading Teacher, 39,* 564–570.

KWLQ: Inquiry and literacy learning in science

Patricia Ruggiano Schmidt

VOLUME 52, NUMBER 7, APRIL 1999

In recent issues *The Reading Teacher* has included articles concerning teacher inquiry into classroom literacy learning and teacher/student collaborative inquiry. "Thinking About Teaching Through Inquiry" (Cousin, Dembrow, & Molldrem-Shamel, 1997) described a cyclical systematic procedure for teacher questions and reflections about classroom practice. The four-step process provided a structure for positive classroom change. In the article "K-W-W-L: Questioning the Known" (Bryan, 1998), a teacher described a classroom process for collaborative unit planning with intermediate-grade elementary students in a midwestern, rural school. She used the K-W-W-L format for building upon students' prior knowledge, so that they could successfully begin generating questions and designing scientific experiments.

Similarly, teachers at two schools in Syracuse, New York, began thinking about teaching through inquiry and developed a framework for their own question generation. However, they used the procedure not only for building upon prior knowledge, but also as a means for recording and generating questions throughout the study. Additionally, this inquiry learning provided authentic opportunities for students to develop their literacy learning.

Due to a district initiative and feelings of inadequacy about teaching science, the teachers profiled here attended an inquiry learning staff development workshop where they learned that inquiry learning and teaching is based on a constructivist approach (Confrey, 1990; Fosnot, 1996; Piaget, 1970), which views learning as a meaning-making process. For inquiry learning in science, children are presented with firsthand experiences to experiment, solve problems, and discover how the world functions as they question, plan, investigate, reflect, explain, and summarize. Furthermore, during the process, elementary classrooms become sites where literacy learning develops naturally as children formulate questions, explore textual information, record and analyze data, and report findings (Peck & Hughes, 1996; Schmidt, 1999).

After the workshop, the teachers began designing and teaching inquiry lessons. They discovered that through inquiry lessons students maintained focus, had many positive social interactions, and went well beyond teacher objectives for learning. However, they noted that during the early stages of inquiry, children had great difficulty generating their own questions for study. Teachers questioned:

"I know a key component of inquiry learning is student-generated questions, but how do you encourage children to take the initiative?"

"Some students ask questions that don't seem to involve much thought. How do you get students to ask higher level questions?"

"How can they learn to ask their own questions while gathering and analyzing data?"

A key component in scientific inquiry is that questioning occurs throughout the inquiry learning process (Chaille & Britain, 1991). Questioning serves as a means to drive initial inquiry as well as the means for maintaining the interest needed to sustain the inquiry process. Therefore, students who are capable of asking more questions as they delve into a subject of study frequently demonstrate greater comprehension of the content (Raphael & Pearson, 1985).

After consultation, discussion, and reflection with workshop leaders, the teachers began using a modified version of Ogle's (1986) K-W-L for reading comprehension. They added a Q, and the resulting KWLQ became a useful strategy to help children frame questions in a consistent format throughout inquiry units of study. For *K, what I know*, students recorded prior knowledge of a topic. For *W, what I want to learn*, they generated questions about the topic. Next, the students read, talked to people, visited places, viewed videos, and explored the Internet to find answers to their questions. For *L, what I learned*, the students recorded and explained aloud the information discovered. Finally, *Q* encouraged *more questions*, so that students would see that learning is a continuous quest; excellent research should lead to more questions for further study. KWLQ served as a means for creating a questioning atmosphere for systematic recording and reporting. Students constructed meaning as they searched for the answers to their own as well as their classmates' questions. Children in kindergarten and Grades 2 and 5 used KWLQ as they participated in scientific inquiry.

Kindergarten

Donna and Len, a kindergarten teaching team, created an inquiry unit about plants. Their students, in pairs, began examining a variety of seeds. They drew pictures of their seeds and, using invented spellings or telling in teacher transcription, described the seeds. Their work was shared on a wall chart labeled "What I *Know*."

The teachers listed the following:

What I *Know*

These are red beans.

These are round green seeds.

This is rice.

I know this is corn.

These are yellow seeds.

These are brown seeds.

These are white and round and hard.

Mine has a funny white thing on the end.

These are from watermelon.

The next day, Donna and Len led a discussion about the seeds and then encouraged the children to ask questions about the seeds. Len explained, "There are many words that begin questions, such as *who*, *what*, *where*, *when*, *why*, and *how*; there are many other ways too! Let's take turns asking questions." The teachers modeled, and the children began to ask questions. They prompted when necessary and then asked, "Why do we ask questions?" The children quickly responded with, "I want answers!" "To find out stuff." "To get some help." Finally, Donna and Len challenged them to ask questions about their seeds and recorded questions on another chart, labeled "What Do I *Want* to Learn?"

What Do I *Want* to Learn?

Will they grow?

Are they apple seeds?

How about pumpkin seeds?

Can we eat them?

Where will my seed grow?

How big will the plants be?

Is it pumpkin seed?

Who plants seeds?

Do they need water?

What do they need to grow?

How about sunshine?

Why does mine have a funny white thing on the end?

How do you cook them?

Initially, the children asked more than 20 questions and added daily to the class list. The teachers informed them that they might find answers to their questions at home, in books, from guests, on walks, in class, and on special trips.

Through classroom inquiry activities such as planting seeds in cups around the room, reading picture books, watching videos, and visiting apple and pumpkin farms, children discovered answers to their questions and recorded them on a third hanging chart, "What I *Learned*."

What I *Learned*

Seeds need dirt.

Seeds need sun and water to grow.

Some seeds don't grow, because they are too old.

Seeds grow to be big and little plants, just like people.

Seeds are food for us.

That funny little white thing is the beginning of a baby plant.

They need sun to stay green and grow big.

They get food from the dirt and water.

The green on the plant is chlorophyll.

The sun helps the plant make food.

Seeds need light after they come out of the dirt.

Some plants don't have to have light. Mushrooms are like that.

Put seeds in boiling water and cook them for soup.

Many more answers were found and recorded. Children also kept journals in which they drew their own plants growing from seeds in cups. They measured their plants and predicted growth. Several children planted more than one seed in a cup and discovered the need to transplant. They also asked questions about plant parts and the best conditions for growing their plants.

Near the end of 3 weeks, the class reviewed the answers to their questions and began thinking of more questions to ask. Donna and Len stated that they could find answers when they had free time at home or in the classroom. They could share their answers with the class. Their questions were written on another chart entitled "More *Questions*."

More *Questions*

Will my plant grow beans that I can eat?

Can I grow a garden?

What plants can I grow at home?

Can we grow a garden outside by the school?

How do plants get so big, like trees?

Where are the biggest and smallest plants?

How long does it take seeds to grow to plants?

The K, W, L, and Q charts guided study as Donna and Len planned for their daily lessons. Children read the charts to each other and as a class. The teachers and the children discovered that the charts not only acted as a means for developing literacy learning, but also served as organizational tools for inquiry.

Second grade

Susan's second-grade class began their unit of study with a class discussion about insects. They recorded information on a class chart entitled *What I Know About Insects*. Next, they listed questions concerning what they wanted to learn about insects on a chart entitled, *What I Want to Know About Insects*. They then watched a video about insects in their region of the country and recorded answers to questions learned from the video on another chart entitled, *What I Learned About Insects*. Finally they looked at the unanswered questions and considered the sources necessary to find the answers, such as, from "real, live" insects, from people and books at home or in school, from the library, from entomologists, from farmers, and from the Internet. Throughout the unit, they also added questions to the chart entitled *More Questions About Insects*.

During the unit, children in pairs chose an insect and searched for information. While exploring, they completed a KWLQ chart for the insect. Katie and Lonnie (pseudonyms), two children with special needs in literacy learning, generated questions and recorded the answers discovered during their research about butterflies. As they read books about butterflies and talked to each other, they took turns recording the information. They also selected the Monarch butterfly to draw, color, and label parts: head, thorax, abdomen, six legs, wings, and antennae. When they shared their findings with the whole class, they proudly read their chart and explained their picture. KWLQ chart in Table 1 shows their work.

Daily the second-grade children added more questions and answers to the class chart and were proud to see the many unanswered questions. As one insightful child declared, "This means we can keep asking questions and find answers all year." Susan made the insect chart a permanent display as children continued discovering, questioning, and sharing.

Fifth grade

The fifth-grade students began using KWLQ charts individually and in pairs for a unit about pond life. Each child drew four columns on a standard sheet of notebook paper. Cindy and Mary, the teaching team, briefly instructed about the KWLQ format. Then, the children listed under K what they know about pond life and read their recorded prior knowledge in small groups. Next, Cindy led a brief discussion about questions and asked them to create their own questions about pond life under their W column. The teachers encouraged them to explore the literature on pond life that they had collected for the class. The children added to the K columns on their charts and shared their many questions

---

Table 1
Katie and Lonnie's KWLQ chart

What I Know	What Do I Want To Find Out?
I know Butter FLY's are pirrett. They are in SUMMer.	Do Butterfly's eat? From flowers Do they Bit? No Do they have Baby's? Yes, FRom EGGs

What I Learned	More Questions
have black and oeige (orange) they are clld Monarch they fold wing's to sleep they fly rnd the Day thy fly 2000 Aiewrs (hours) it is diffet (different) to a butterfly to mohe (moth) Sometime a butterfly's red yellw	How big can they grew? How long to liv? How many Baby's? where do they liv? why do they di?

Table 2
Ponds and pond life KWLQ chart

K	W	L	Q
1. filled with water	How does water get in?	from underground springs and rains.	Can we skate on the pond in winter?
2. ducks	How big?	euglena, and other plants make it green.	Why do snails eat algae?
3. fish	How did it get here?	snakes, turtles.	Why do ponds die?
4. frogs	Why are ponds green?	just like the seasons.	How big are leeches?
5. lily pads	What kind of reptiles?	water boatman, dragonflies, musqitoes and water fleas.	Why do frogs make bubbles?
6. reptiles	Does the temperature change?	ameoba, paramecium are one celled animals.	Why do plants turn to soil?
7. muddy	What insects are there?	amphibians like frogs.	What happens in winter?
8. not too hot or cold	What other plants and animals?	leeches, snails.	How do they live in the ice?
9. many different insects	Why do some plants have legs?	cilia help them swim.	What lives or dies?

with the whole class. They also thought of where they could find more answers. Other library books, scientists, wildlife experts, television, and a local pond were all mentioned.

The following day, the class walked a few miles to the pond, maintained as a wildlife preserve in an urban setting, and began to discover answers. When they returned to the classroom, they recorded answers to some questions under the L column, and added more questions under the W. They left the Q column blank, saving it for final research questions. They were then given time to read class re-

sources for more information and were advised that a naturalist would be visiting soon. At that time, more questions could be answered and asked.

When the children believed they had found most of the answers to their questions, they began talking with a partner about their research report using the chart. They also added questions to the Q column. These were the questions left unanswered that might be answered in the future. Table 2 is an example of a KWLQ chart completed by a typical fifth-grade student in this class.

The student who recorded information in this chart ended with why questions, which seemed to show a more complex level of understanding than her original questions (Raphael & Pearson, 1985).

When the children finished sharing information and recording on their KWLQ charts, they wrote reports. The introduction of the reports included information from the first column, K. The second paragraph included a few of the student's favorite questions from W. The next paragraphs discussed the answers to their questions from L. The concluding paragraph incorporated statements, opinions, and conjectures that students wanted to make about their research as well as the final questions from Q, questions that had been left unanswered but could be studied in the future. Students, individually and in pairs, read their reports to the class and placed them on a literature table next to the wall containing the huge pond life mural, sketched and painted by all class members.

Formulating questions and literacy learning

At the heart of inquiry learning is questioning, but student ability to ask questions about content is often based on prior knowledge (Raphael & Pearson, 1985; Rumelhart, 1980). Therefore, the teacher must act as the facilitator who sets broad objectives, plans experiences to help students establish basic knowledge, gathers materials and resources,

models questioning behaviors, and guides discovery processes (Birnie & Ryan, 1984; Hawkins, 1965). On the basis of previous personal and school experiences and connected to new experiences, kindergarten, second-grade, and fifth-grade students questioned and discovered through KWLQ. First, they recorded their prior knowledge; then they formulated, recorded, and reported questions; next, they searched for answers through reading and firsthand experiences and recorded and reported their answers; finally, they noted more questions for further study. As the teachers anticipated specific answers based on the units of study, the students responded with not only those answers, but information beyond what the curriculum required. KWLQ provides a compelling framework for question formulation and discovery and practice for literacy learning as children naturally connect reading, writing, listening, and speaking for authentic inquiry learning.

REFERENCES

Birnie, H.H., & Ryan, A. (1984). Inquiry discovery revisited. *Science and Children, 21*(7), 31–34.

Bryan, J. (1998). K-W-W-L: Questioning the known. *The Reading Teacher, 51,* 618–620.

Chaille, C., & Britain, L. (1991). *The young child as scientist: A constructivist approach to early childhood science education.* New York: HarperCollins

Confrey, J. (1990). What constructivism implies for teaching. In R.B. Davis, C.A. Maher, & N. Noddings (Eds.), *Constructivist views on the teaching and learning of mathematics* (pp. 107–122). Reston, VA: National Council of Teachers of Mathematics.

Cousin, P.T., Dembrow, M.P., & Molldrem-Shamel, J. (1997). Inquiry about learners and learning: Thinking about teaching through inquiry. *The Reading Teacher, 51*, 162–164.

Fosnot, C. (1996). *Constructivism: Theory, perspectives and practice.* New York: Teachers College Press.

Hawkins, D. (1965), Messing about in science. *Science and Children, 2*, 5–9.

Ogle, D.M. (1986). K-W-L: A teaching model that develops active reading of expository text. *The Reading Teacher, 39*, 564–570.

Peck, J.K., & Hughes, S.V. (1996). *Inquiry pedagogy: Maximizing literacy learning and teaching through shared inquiry.* Paper presented at the annual meeting of the American Educational Research Association, New York.

Piaget, J. (1970). *The science of education and the psychology of the child.* New York: Orion Press.

Raphael, T.E., & Pearson, P.D. (1985). Increasing student awareness of sources of information for answering questions. *American Educational Research Journal, 22*, 217–237.

Rumelhart, D. (1980). Schemata: The building blocks of cognition. In R.J. Spiro, B.C. Bruce & W.F. Brewer (Eds.), *Theoretical issues in reading comprehension* (pp. 33–58). Hillsdale, NJ: Erlbaum.

Schmidt, P.R. (1999) *Reading, writing, listening, and speaking through scientific inquiry: Six diverse learners respond.* Manuscript submitted for publication.

K-W-L-S

Arne E. Sippola

VOLUME 48, NUMBER 6, MARCH 1995

K-W-L (Carr & Ogle, 1987; Heller, 1986; Ogle, 1986, 1992) is a popular activity for assisting students in activating background knowledge, structuring inquiry, and summarizing learned information. The *K* represents what students already know about a particular topic, and the *W* represents what students want to know about the topic. Notes about both of these are recorded on a three-column chart before students read. After reading, students enter in the third (*L*) column what they learned about the topic.

Ogle (1986) originally included two categories of information to be recorded in the third column: What I learned and what I still need to learn. In my work with children, I noticed that they frequently emphasized the "what I learned" component of the third column and minimized the content of "what I still need to learn." Although the two are certainly linked, it would seem clearer for children if they

K-W-L-S			
What I already know	What I want to know	What I learned	What I still need to learn

were charted as two separate categories. Thus, I developed K-W-L-S, which is essentially identical to K-W-L with an added fourth column: "what I still need to learn." In this way, readers may attend to what remains unanswered and is worth further inquiry after reading.

The results have been positive. Elementary students include much more "what I still need to learn" information on the four-column chart as compared to the traditional K-W-L chart. K-W-L-S focuses readers' attention more directly upon "what I still need to know" information.

REFERENCES

Carr, E., & Ogle, D. (1987). KWL plus: A strategy for comprehension and summarization. *Journal of Reading, 30,* 626–631.

Heller, M. (1986). How do you know what you know? Metacognitive modeling in the content areas. *Journal of Reading, 29,* 415–422.

Ogle, D. (1986). KWL: A teaching model that develops active reading of expository text. *The Reading Teacher, 39,* 564–570.

Ogle, D. (1992). KWL in action: Secondary teachers find applications that work. In E.K. Dishner, T.W. Bean, J.E. Readance, & D.W. Moore (Eds.), *Reading in the content areas: Improving classroom instruction* (3rd ed., pp. 270–281). Dubuque, IA: Kendall/Hunt.

Using K-W-L for informal assessment

Patricia J. McAllister

VOLUME 47, NUMBER 6, MARCH 1994

K-W-L (Know, Want to Know, Learned; Ogle, 1986) has become a popular technique for teaching students how to learn from informational texts. We regularly use this process with our compensatory education students in the first, second, and third grades. However, we sometimes notice that several students respond frequently while others respond sporadically or not at all. We needed a process to keep track of responders and nonresponders so that we could better analyze students' progress.

As a result, I developed a procedure for keeping a record of the quality and quantity of student responses. Since I put the K-W-L charts and all of the responses on large chart paper, the procedure first involves putting students' names or initials after their contributions during the discussions. We noticed that more students began to volunteer during the discussions and appeared to be taking ownership of their responses of the charts.

After each lesson, we transfer information from each chart to the two forms that I developed to document and analyze group and individual progress (see Figures 1 and 2). These allow us to see our students' progress and needs.

In analyzing the responses, we give a Good rating for more than one response, an Average rating for one response, and a Poor rating for no participation during any part of the discussion. A Comments column allows us to note important information related to quality of responses or participation during a discussion.

Tallying the number of responses provides a picture of the GAP (*Good*, *Average*, *Poor*) between what our students actually do and what we want them to be able to accomplish. We then jot down summary statements and note students' needs at the bottom of the form. From this analysis, we are able to plan better lessons for groups and pay more attention to individual students.

The process of analyzing total group and individual progress affords us many opportunities to consider the effects of background knowledge on students' learning, ways to encourage reluctant participants, and ways to meet students' individ-

---

ual needs. Looking at students in this manner also enables us to discuss progress in a more knowledgeable manner with classroom teachers. Classroom teachers receive the Group Record of Responses at least three times during the year so that they can see their students' progress. The Individual Record of Responses is placed

Figure 1
K-W-L group record of responses

Topic: _Trees_   Date: _4-3-91_

\# = Number of responses

Good (G), Average (A), Poor (P) = Quality of responses

Group _Second Grade_

Student	#K	K	#W	W	#L	L	Comments
Ryan	4	G	0	P	3	G	All text-based on L Good background knowledge
Sandy	2	G	0	P	1	A	Good text-based and in-the-head response on L
Mark	2	G	0	P	2	G	Good responses on L Looked back at text!
Robert	2	G	2	G	0	P	Started out good then fizzled. No attention to text.
Janet	0	P	1	A	2	G	Took info for L from text pictures.
Adam	1	A	1	A	0	P	Much participation in the beginning then lost him.
Susan	2	G	3	G	1	A	Good quality responses all through disc.
Michelle	1	A	0	P	0	P	Half asleep but she tried.
Totals		G 5 A 2 P 1		G 2 A 2 P 4		G 3 A 2 P 3	G - 10 A - 6 P - 8

Summary of responses: "Good" and "Average" responses increased over last KWL (Kon). Students are becoming more confident.

Needs of students: Refer Janet to text print as well as pictures. Continue to encourage Michelle, Adam and Robert. Focus on how to ask questions related to the topic.

Figure 2
K-W-L individual record of responses

= Number of responses

Good (G), Average (A), Poor (P) = Quality of responses

Student ___Susan S.___   Grade ___2___

Topic	Date	#K	K	#W	W	#L	L	Comments
Weather	9-15-91	0	P	0	P	0	P	No interest or fear of responding?
Rain	11-12-91	1	A	0	P	2	G	Better participation skimmed text for L
Trees	4-3-91	2	G	3	G	3	G	Good quality responses all through discussion
Totals		G 1 A 1 P 1		G 1 A 0 P 2		G 2 A 0 P 1	G 4 A 1 P 4	

Summary of overall responses: Susan has made progress in her willingness to participate and refer to text.

Needs of student: Continue to encourage her. Teach additional fix-up strategies to use with text.

in each student's compensatory education file as part of his or her progress report.

The process of using ongoing instruction for documentation and analysis enables us to formulate more accurate views of our students and to increase the dialogue between the compensatory education staff and classroom teachers.

REFERENCE

Ogle, D.M. (1986). K-W-L: A teaching model that develops active reading of expository text. *The Reading Teacher, 39,* 564–570.

Teaching nonfiction with the shared book experience

Jill E. Scott

VOLUME 47, NUMBER 8, MAY 1994

Children's literature has increasingly become an important feature of the elementary classroom. It is encouraging that more teachers are moving toward literature-based curricula. However, as fiction is used more extensively and teachers concentrate on collecting quality fiction for their classroom libraries, it is important to remember nonfiction as a valuable tool in teaching students about books and reading.

The new nonfiction

Elleman (1992) mentions that often we think of fiction as a way to excite children about books, yet we need to realize that nonfiction is the genre some children prefer. We should not forget the "fascination of facts" (Vardell & Copeland, 1992, p. 76). Informational books have changed; they are not just for research reports anymore.

Nonfiction literature is awash in fresh, new titles and bigger and better illustrations and photographs. Fortunately, in recent years more nonfiction titles have been published, with many available in paperback. We have "a bold profusion of nonfiction titles, books written by authors who care about their subject and produced by publishers who treat each book as an addition to our body of literature" (Greenlaw, 1992, p. 46). Nonfiction books by Seymour Simon, Joanna Cole, Patricia Lauber, Dorothy Hinshaw Patent, Milton Meltzer, James Cross Giblin, Mitsumasa Anno, and Aliki are worth investigating.

Shared book experience

One of the most exciting and effective methods of sharing literature with children is the shared book experience. First developed by Don Holdaway (1979) of New Zealand, this method not only allows children to hear a story read aloud, but also fosters participation in the story.

Shared book experience stimulates literacy and has been used successfully in many primary classrooms with fiction. It allows young children to read the first day of school and is a fine vehicle for capturing the teachable moment. These characteristics are as crucial to nonfiction as they are to fiction.

We need to use more nonfiction in our classrooms, and shared book experience is one good way to incorporate its use.

Shared book experience and nonfiction

Shared book experience in my first-grade classroom includes several books of fiction, poetry, songs, and at least one non-fiction book each day. Forty minutes a day is set aside for this part of the curriculum. Although many of the nonfiction books we use relate to a science or social studies theme, not all do. Just as with fiction, non-fiction can be read simply for enjoyment.

Let's Visit a Television Station, text by Carol Freed and photography by Larry French (Troll Associates, 1988), is one book I read with my students recently. We were not doing a unit related to this book; I simply thought that my students could relate to its topic and that it had the potential to extend their knowledge about television. I also chose the book because it was written in an easily understood style and contained attractive and inform-ative photographs.

I began our shared book experience by rereading a requested storybook from the previous day. We then read some poems that were posted around the room and sang a song we had been using to review letter sounds. I introduced a new fic-tion big book that we read three times, with students' participation increasing

with each reading. Then I brought out *Let's Visit a Television Station*.

Shared book experience with SQ3R

When using a nonfiction book with the class, I often apply the SQ3R strategy. While SQ3R is commonly used with non-fiction and especially textbooks, I find it helpful to use orally during shared book experience. As described in Holdaway (1980) and extended to meet the needs of an oral shared book experience, the steps of SQ3R are:

1. Survey–Preview. Note the format of the book and discuss children's previous knowledge of the topic.

2. Question. Make predictions and pose questions inspired by the preview.

3. Read. In the case of shared book ex-perience, read the book orally with the teacher leading. The book may be reread if students desire.

4. Recite. Answer or discuss questions generated earlier. More questions may be asked.

5. Review. State the main idea, recall-ing and revisiting the text to assure com-prehension.

The steps of SQ3R have been used of-ten throughout the school year in my classroom with both fiction and nonfic-tion, so as I displayed the new nonfiction book, the students immediately began to make comments about the cover. The photo and title were clear indicators of the book's topic. The children were excited at the thought of being able to talk about television as we began our shared book experience lesson, using the SQ3R strategy.

Survey—We looked through the book, paying attention to the photographs and noting the location of the text and the length of the book. I asked questions to discover what the children already knew about television: How do television shows suddenly appear on your TV at home? How is a television show made? How do television shows and motion pictures compare?

The discussion was then allowed to include personal stories about the children's televisions at home and their TV viewing habits. Some questions posed were: What are your favorite television shows? What do you like about them? How often do you watch TV? Have you ever been to a television station? What do you think it would be like? Do you prefer going to the movies or watching a video on TV? Why?

Questions continued as they were brought up by the children. After about 5 minutes, we summarized what we knew and liked about television, and then we were ready to delve into the book.

Question—Prediction was our next task, and it was easily done with this particular book. I asked: What do you think this book will be about? What do the pictures tell you? What do you know already that you think will be mentioned in this book? What do you want to learn?

Let's Visit a Television Station has an excellent introductory paragraph, so I read it to the students and asked them to come up with specific questions they thought would be answered by the book. Some questions generated were: What are some of the things found in a television station? What is it like to work there? Is it fun? What equipment do you need to put a show on television? Where is a television station we can visit?

These questions were copied onto chart paper or on the chalkboard to be discussed after the book was read.

Read—I read the book aloud the first time through. During subsequent readings, the students joined in. Words and sentences were highlighted for work on phonics, word attack strategies, conventions of print, and vocabulary enrichment. The words were then put back into context, and the book was read again as a piece of nonfiction literature.

Recite—After reading, the students were directed to the questions they generated before the book was read. Information from answered questions was written on chart paper or on the chalkboard next to the question. For unanswered questions we discussed where to get the answer. More questions were asked at this time: What are some specific jobs at a television station? Would you like to work at a television station? Is putting on a television show difficult?

Review—Some questions that directed this part of the shared book experience were: What was the most important thing about the book? What will you remember about the book? What did you already know? What did you learn? Why did the author include a particular section? Did this book have the information you wanted? Why did the photographer choose to include the photo on page three? Were there enough photographs? What other photographs do you think should have been included? Would you like to read another book on the subject? Why or why not?

Extending shared book experience

To conclude the shared book experience with a nonfiction book, students were offered the opportunity to give their opinions of the book. Students responded that they were a little disappointed in it. Although they felt they had learned about television stations, they still wanted to know more about their favorite shows. They also mentioned that they wished the book had discussed cartoon shows.

As I plan extension activities for a book (some books we read simply for pleasure and discussion, others we follow up because they pique our interest or bring up other topics or issues), I always follow the children's interests and questions.

In the case of *Let's Visit a Television Station*, the children wanted more information about television shows. I took the opportunity to take them to the school library to look for more books. We used the encyclopedias and the card catalog and sifted through the information together. Still not finding what they wanted, the students decided to write their own books on TV and include facts about their favorite TV shows.

Other possible extensions for shared nonfiction include:

• Reading the book into a tape recorder and making the tape and book available in a listening center.

• Using drama to enhance the new information the students have learned. We might have produced our own TV show after reading *Let's Visit a Television Station*.

• Creating art work to reproduce information acquired from nonfiction literature. For example, if we were producing our own TV show, we might also have wanted to construct a large screen television out of cardboard.

• Using the words from the nonfiction book in a class-made big book. The students could add their own illustrations or photos. The big book could then be easily used for individual and choral readings and lessons on conventions of print.

• Taking words from nonfiction literature for vocabulary study, phonics study, and spelling. My first graders learned why TV is short for television, and we made lists of words ending in *ion*, like *television* and *station*.

Children should love nonfiction as much as they love fiction. In our classrooms, where fiction plays a precious role in educating students, nonfiction needs to have a role as well. Shared book experience can emphasize the immense pleasure that can be gleaned from books, both fiction and nonfiction. Fiction can take children into the world of make-believe and self-discovery. Nonfiction can take them into the world of new ideas, interesting facts, and possibilities for the future. Both worlds are enjoyable, attainable, and necessary for our students to become literate, well-informed, joyous readers.

REFERENCES

Elleman, B. (1992). The nonfiction scene: What's happening? In E.B. Freeman & D.G. Person (Eds.), *Using nonfiction trade books in the elementary classroom: From ants to zeppelins* (pp. 26–33). Urbana, IL: National Council of Teachers of English.

Greenlaw, M.J. (1992). Interacting with informational books. In B. Cullinan (Ed.), *Invitation to read: More children's literature in the reading program* (pp. 40–47). Newark, DE: International Reading Association.

Holdaway, D. (1979). *The foundations of literacy*. Gosford, NSW, Australia: Ashton Scholastic.

Holdaway, D. (1980). *Independence in reading*. Portsmouth, NH: Heinemann.

Vardell, S.M., & Copeland, K.A. (1992). Reading aloud and responding to nonfiction: Let's talk about it. In E.B. Freeman & D.G. Person (Eds.), *Using nonfiction trade books in the elementary classroom: From ants to zeppelins* (pp. 76–85). Urbana, IL: National Council of Teachers of English.

Using graphic organizers to improve the reading of mathematics

Stephania Braselton
Barbara C. Decker

VOLUME 48, NUMBER 3, NOVEMBER 1994

Mathematics is the most difficult content area material to read because there are more concepts per word, per sentence, and per paragraph than in any other subject (Brennan & Dunlap, 1985; Culyer, 1988; Thomas, 1988). Reading mathematics is complex because of the mixture of words, numerals, letters, symbols, and graphics that require the reader to shift from one type of vocabulary to another. To complicate matters further, examination of mathematics textbooks reveals that the math concepts presented may be appropriate to the grade level for which the books are designed; however, the reading level of the text is often 1, 2, or even 3 years above the level of the population for which the text is intended (Brennan & Dunlap, 1985). Often students have not been taught the variety of reading skills necessary for comprehending mathematics materials. Specialized reading of mathematics is so essential that a study by Maffei (1973) showed that reading teachers were more successful than experienced mathematics teachers in teaching students to solve word problems.

One strategy that is effective in improving content area reading comprehension is the use of graphic organizers (Clarke, 1991; Flood, Lapp, & Farnan, 1986; Piccolo, 1987). This strategy involves five steps. First, the student must restate the problem question. A student who can explain a problem in his or her own words has conceptualized the situation being described and is more likely to be successful with subsequent steps of the problem-solving process.

Next, the student must decide what information is necessary for solving the problem. These data may appear directly in the problem or may have to be computed from the data that are given. Any extra information that appears in the problem should be eliminated at this stage.

After the necessary information has been retrieved, the graphic organizer provides a third step for planning the mathematical calculations that must be performed. During this step, the student must attend not only to the necessary mathematical operations but also to the sequence in which the operations should take place.

At the fourth stage, the student actually performs the calculations necessary for solving the word problem. By the time this step is reached, the student has clearly defined the problem, selected the necessary information, and planned a logical sequence of mathematical steps leading to the solution. The student is then free to focus on the mathematical skills involved in the solution.

The final step leads the student back to a more holistic view of the problem-solving process. At this stage, the student asks himself/herself if the answer computed is reasonable. In order to do this, the student must review the previous steps in the graphic organizer. In addition, the problem data and solution must be compared.

Since the strength of graphic organizers lies in their ability to visually relate elements of a story (or story problem), layout and design are important. A diamond shape (see Figure 1) reinforces the fact that each student begins a word problem with the same information and, when successful, arrives at the same conclusion upon completion of the problem. However, between these two points students should be encouraged to think divergently in order to make full use of the wide variety of problem-solving strategies available to them.

Teaching the organizer

This graphic organizer was used with my (Stephania's) fifth graders, who typically had not read word problems for meaning. Instead, they scanned the passages to find key words like *in all*, *total*, *left*, and *remain*, and then looked at the numerical relationships of the numbers to decide which operations to use. Students needed help taking a more holistic view of word problems.

Instruction in problem solving began by teaching strategies that would help students read word problems as meaningful passages. Problems were selected that would reflect experiences familiar to most of the students. The situations set forth in each problem were read and discussed; when possible, students acted out the events described. Students were encouraged to write, rewrite, and discuss word problem solutions in their learning logs. They were encouraged to think of each problem as a short story from which they could make meaning by using their prior experience.

Modeling

The next step was to introduce the graphic organizer. First, students were shown a transparency of the graphic organizer, and each of the steps in the organizer was discussed. Students were

Figure 1
Graphic organizer

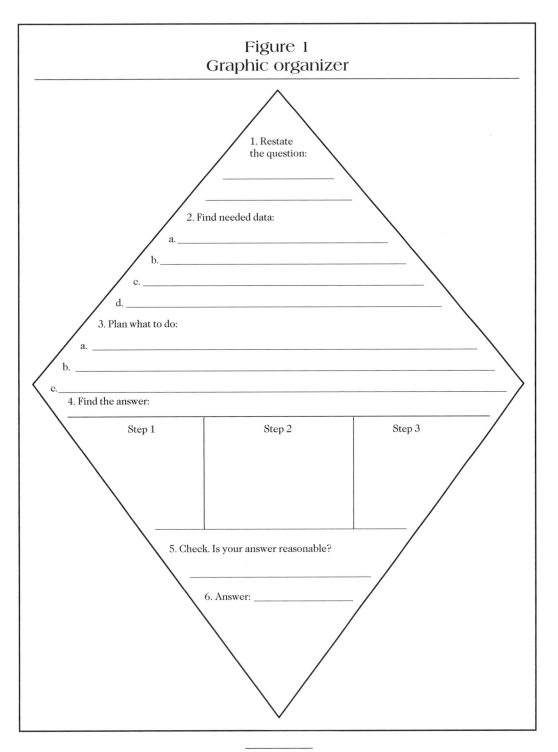

1. Restate
the question:

_____

_____

2. Find needed data:

a. _____

b. _____

c. _____

d. _____

3. Plan what to do:

a. _____

b. _____

c. _____

4. Find the answer:

Step 1	Step 2	Step 3

5. Check. Is your answer reasonable?

_____

6. Answer: _____

asked to describe how each step would help in solving a story problem.

Once students were familiar with the format of the organizer, the following story problem was modeled:

Justin has a collection of 36 baseball caps. He began collecting them when he was 7 years old, and he collected the same number each year. If he is now 16, how many caps did he collect each year?

I began by reading the word problem and doing a think-aloud as I worked on the first step of the organizer. During the think-aloud, I talked about what I knew from my own experience about baseball caps and about collecting as a hobby. Then I asked students how they could use their own experiences to understand narrative material.

After reading the problem and accessing prior knowledge, I modeled the first step of the organizer, restating the question. I wanted students to understand that putting the question into their own words would help them comprehend what the problem was asking. We compared restatements such as: "How many caps did he collect each year?" "How many caps has he collected each year since he was 7?" "How many caps did he collect each year between the ages of 7 and 16?" The students all agreed that the last restatement was the clearest. After we restated the problem in this way, a number of students were eager to move on to the next steps because they felt confident that they knew how to approach the problem solution.

After the students seemed to understand the problem question, I modeled and discussed Step 2 of the graphic organizer. I demonstrated how I first looked at the problem holistically and ascertained that I had to know how many years Justin had been collecting caps and how many caps he had collected in all. Then I noted that while the latter information was directly stated, the number of years Justin had been collecting was not given. (If students have to look further for information from which the needed data can be computed, this information should be listed in Step 2. If not, the problem solver must either find the information elsewhere or terminate problem-solving efforts.)

By the time I was ready to model Step 3 of the organizer, most of the students had a clear idea of the steps needed to solve the problem. I modeled the two-step process of computing the number of years Justin had been collecting and then determined how many caps he must have collected each year.

Because the mathematics involved in the problem were so simple, there was little need to spend a great deal of time modeling Step 4. I kept the mathematics simple so as not to impede students' problem-solving efforts.

Although checking reasonableness of an answer (Step 5) seems like a simple process, I have found that few students evaluate their answers in this way. Some students simply do not think to do this. Others have difficulty with the estimation skills necessary to make such a global analysis or lack the experiential background to determine what is reasonable. I began Step 5 by showing students examples of some incorrect solutions to the problem based upon errors in a similar problem. In each case, I asked the students to tell whether the answer seemed reasonable and to explain why. Since the problem information had been thoroughly discussed and recorded on the organizer, students had little difficulty seeing that these solutions yielded answers that were unreasonable.

Guided practice

When the students' responses indicated readiness, copies of the organizer were provided, and students were guided through each step of the problem-solving process. They were encouraged to give reasons for the responses they wrote on their organizer and to discuss what they were thinking as they read the problems. These discussions gave students exposure to different approaches to the same problem and reinforced the idea that they could think divergently, yet still arrive at the correct solution. Less able math students benefited from hearing how their peers applied prior experience in order to make sense of the word problem.

Independent practice

As students became more confident in their use of the organizer, they moved from teacher-guided problem solving to working in small groups. The small group setting gave more opportunity for individual input and encouraged less confident students to participate. Group discussions helped students to clarify their thinking about a variety of problem-solving situations.

Students had the most difficulty with problems containing extra information. Many of them assumed that all the information contained in a word problem must be used in its solution. This obstacle was overcome by comparing these types of problems with students' previous encounters with narrative reading. We discussed how authors use detailed descriptions of characters in order to help the reader form mental images, although these details are not always essential to understanding the story conflict or its resolution. Students realized that an author may give information that is related to a problem-solving situation but is not essential to the solution of the problem, so readers must use their own experience and knowledge of mathematical concepts to determine whether or not a particular piece of information is needed.

For several days, I allotted a few minutes of math time to solving a word problem using the organizer. We solved a variety of problems, including some that had extra information and some that could be solved in more than one way. I wanted students to see that the organizer was a guide, not a pat formula for solving problems. Several students using the same organizer could approach a problem in different ways and still get the correct solution.

Results

After engaging in independent practice with the graphic organizer, students showed marked improvement in problem solving. This strategy was effective with students of all ability levels.

Students seemed to benefit most from the more systematic approach to analyzing story problems. Because of their lack of success with word problems, many had developed a habit of making cursory attempts at problem solving. The organizer seemed to provide them with a framework that gave them confidence in their ability to be successful and also required them to think through problem situations before beginning mathematical calculations.

Discussion and conclusion

Several factors accounted for the effectiveness of the graphic organizer. Of most significance was the fact that the organizer required students to slow down and think through each problem. At first, students with more impulsive learning styles resisted the slower process, but they accepted the organizer as they saw their improved performance and ability to successfully solve problems.

The organizer was also effective because students with weak problem-solving skills saw visual organization of the problem-solving process. Also, completion of the organizer required that students express in written language their understanding of the problem-solving process. As students worked together to

do this, they were exposed to different ways of approaching the same problems, and the language expression led to further development of the students' problem-solving schemata.

Those students who had well developed problem-solving skills were less likely to need the graphic organizer in order to be successful in their problem-solving efforts. However, the group setting provided these students with an opportunity to verbalize what they knew and allowed them to process their knowledge at a deeper level. Less able students benefited from hearing how these students approached problem-solving situations.

Figures 2 and 3 show examples of one student's use of the graphic organizer. Initially she was unable to distinguish between essential and extraneous information. The same student using the graphic organizer was later able to solve problems, although she did make one error in transferring her answer from the organizer to the test.

Many of the reading strategies that work in content areas like social studies and science may also be effective in reading mathematics. Language plays an integral role in the processing of concepts, and mathematics is no exception. By using strategies that integrate both language and mathematics skills we can increase students' abilities to function as independent problem solvers. The use of a graphic organizer is an effective strategy that can be added to a repertoire of aids for student problem solving.

Figure 2
Student's use of the graphic organizer

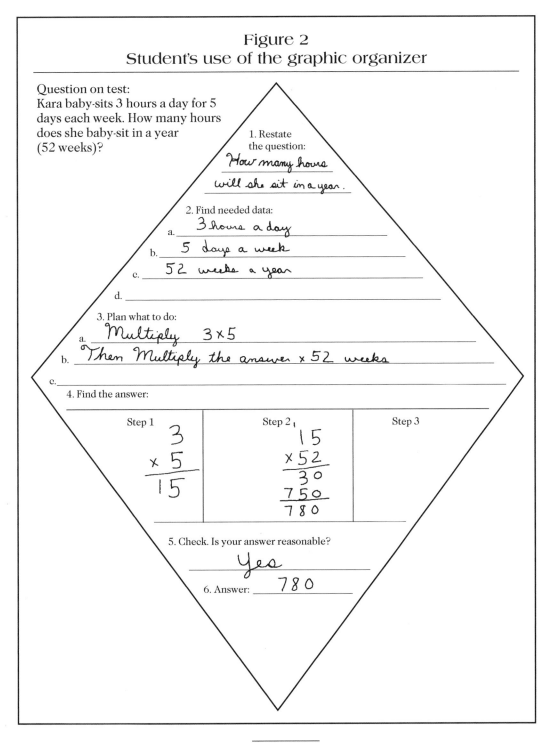

Question on test:
Kara baby-sits 3 hours a day for 5 days each week. How many hours does she baby-sit in a year (52 weeks)?

1. Restate the question:

How many hours will she sit in a year.

2. Find needed data:

a. 3 hours a day

b. 5 days a week

c. 52 weeks a year

d.

3. Plan what to do:

a. Multiply 3 × 5

b. Then Multiply the answer × 52 weeks

c.

4. Find the answer:

Step 1	Step 2	Step 3
3 × 5 15	15 × 52 30 750 780	

5. Check. Is your answer reasonable?

Yes

6. Answer: 780

Figure 3
Student's use of the graphic organizer

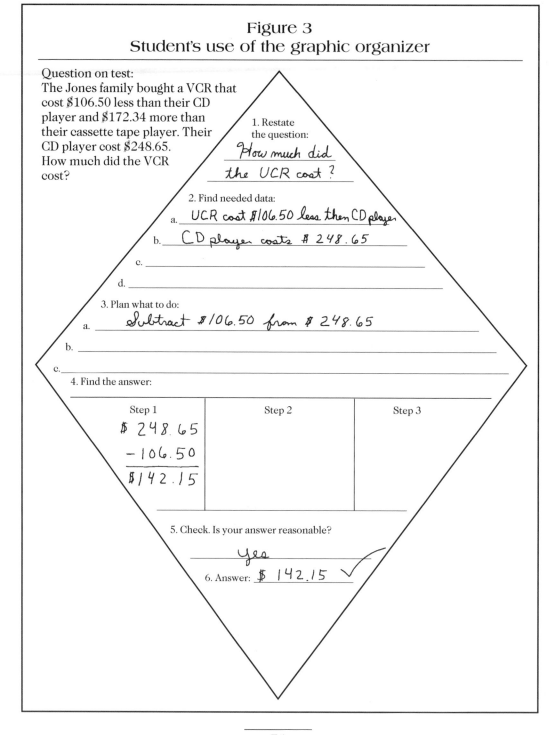

Question on test:
The Jones family bought a VCR that cost $106.50 less than their CD player and $172.34 more than their cassette tape player. Their CD player cost $248.65. How much did the VCR cost?

1. Restate the question:

How much did the UCR cost?

2. Find needed data:
    a. *UCR cost $106.50 less then CD player*
    b. *CD player costs $248.65*
    c. _____
    d. _____

3. Plan what to do:
    a. *Subtract $106.50 from $248.65*
    b. _____
    c. _____

4. Find the answer:

Step 1	Step 2	Step 3
$248.65 −106.50 $142.15		

5. Check. Is your answer reasonable?

Yes

6. Answer: *$142.15* ✓

REFERENCES

Brennan, A.D., & Dunlap, W.P. (1985). What are the prime factors of reading mathematics? *Reading Improvement, 22,* 152–159.

Clarke, J.H. (1991). Using visual organizers to focus on thinking. *Journal of Reading, 34,* 526–534.

Culyer, R.C. (1988). Reading and mathematics go hand in hand. *Reading Improvement, 25,* 189–195.

Flood, J., Lapp, D., & Farnan, N. (1986). A reading-writing procedure that teaches expository paragraph structure. *The Reading Teacher, 39,* 556–562.

Maffei, A.C. (1973). Reading analysis in mathematics. *Journal of Reading, 16,* 546–549.

Piccolo, J.A. (1987). Expository text structure: Teaching and learning strategies. *The Reading Teacher, 40,* 838–847.

Thomas, D.A. (1988). Reading and reasoning skills for math problem solvers. *Journal of Reading, 32,* 244–249.

Beyond retelling the plot: Student-led discussions

Claudia E. Cornett

VOLUME 50, NUMBER 6, MARCH 1997

I sat on the floor with 11 fifth graders ready for the book discussion. They all had a copy of *Tuck Everlasting* (Babbitt, 1975). I smiled as 22 eyes looked to me for the first question. Behind my smile was a grimace: I disliked these weekly meetings that always ended up with students changing my best open questions about the book's themes into chances to retell the plot. It was a mystery to me why I seemed to be the only bored person and how they managed to mislead me every week. That was 8 years ago.

This was a case of productive failure. Beginning with a few simple goals I spent the next years searching for and developing ways to enable students to lead provocative discussions without an adult and to enjoy discussions as much as they enjoyed simple retellings. Based on observations of "real life" book discussions, the following guidelines to teach to students emerged.

Preparing for the discussion

Only students who have read the book can be a part of the book or story dis-cussion. If someone hasn't read the book, the discussion will degenerate into a plot retelling to fill people in on the sequence of events. Once students understand this guideline, the focus shifts to students making a decision to read and be a part of an enjoyable social activity rather than just completing an assignment.

Students read the book and think about ideas to use to start the discussion or to bring up during the discussion. A few examples of ideas include: What was the most *exciting* part? What parts were *puzzling* to you or didn't make sense? What in the book *connects* to your own life in some way? Students jot down page numbers of parts they'd like to read aloud and should be ready to say why they chose these parts.

> Example from *Like Jake and Me* (Jukes, 1984):
>
> Exciting—When the spider got in Jake's clothes because I could just feel how creepy that would be if that happened to me! (p. 17)
>
> Puzzling—I just didn't understand why Jake wouldn't let him help with the wood.

Jake looked like a nice man in the pictures. My dad always likes me to help. (p. 1)

Connecting—I remember when my mom was going to have my little sister. I really was worried and excited at the same time. (p. 3)

Students make a list of *questions* to ask others who have read the book—ones they can't answer. These are important questions that they really want to have others help them answer.

Example from *Officer Buckle and Gloria* (Rathmann, 1995):

1. Why did Gloria not let the policeman see her doing her tricks at first?
2. Why did the author put in the banana pudding accident?

Students pick out *special words* or *phrases* that catch their attention.

Example from *Tuck Everlasting*:

1. "Great potato of a woman" to describe Mrs. Tuck
2. "Sliding egg yolk" to describe the setting sun

Students decide what they think are *truths* in the book that help them to understand people and the world. They put these thoughts in sentences and tell why they are true.

Example from *Officer Buckle and Gloria*:

1. Working with a friend can make what you do better than just working by yourself. It's like you can't ride a teeter-totter by yourself.
2. You have to get people's attention for them to learn anything. I have had teachers who put you to sleep by just telling you stuff and never smiling or having fun like Gloria did.

Setting up the discussion

My goal is to get students to the point where they can meet in small groups of 4–6 children and have a 15–20-minute discussion without the teacher. To reach that point these teaching strategies are helpful.

Use the fishbowl technique in which a small group carries on a discussion while the rest of the students observe. Participate in the discussion at first, and ask for volunteers who feel they have prepared for the discussion. It is helpful to ask students to have written preparation (e.g., a chart in which *exciting*, *puzzling*, and *connecting* ideas are listed). During such a "learning to discuss" discussion, stop periodically and ask the outside circle of observers to comment.

Example:

1. What do people do to keep the discussion going?
2. What can be done to get everyone involved in the discussion?
3. What were things people said that really made sense?

Next, reverse the inner and outer circles and continue the discussion. Use this technique frequently until students understand basic processes such as active listening, creating discussion from others' comments, and asking one another questions for clarification. The quicker you remove yourself from the discussion, the sooner students will talk to one another and not to you.

Once students are ready to have simultaneous small group discussions the teacher can appoint a discussion starter for each group. Soon students learn to rotate this role and feel comfortable volunteering to be the starter.

Sitting on a carpet or at least in a circle facing each other conveys a comfortable egalitarian message that mirrors book discussions outside of school.

Ending the discussion

To help students become discussion facilitators it is helpful to offer some sample discussion "enders." Here are enders that cause students to summarize and allow all students to be involved in the discussion. You may wish to put these on a chart for easy reference. At first students can be asked to simply go around the circle and respond.

Tell one thing you learned in the discussion (e.g., something you did not think about before the discussion).

Tell something someone said that made sense.

Tell the most important ideas brought up or what you'll remember most.

Ask a question you still have.

Tell something you thought of that was like another person's idea.

What a difference! I now look forward to student discussions as much as I do book discussions with friends. I've been delighted with the enthusiasm of students who find, with practice, that they can have a real book discussion and not just convince the teacher they read the book by giving a plot summary. What's more, I hear discussions continue long after the "enders"—in the hall, on the playground, and even in the restrooms!

CHILDREN'S BOOKS CITED

Babbitt, N. (1975). *Tuck everlasting*. New York: Farrar, Straus & Giroux.

Jukes, M. (1984). *Like Jake and me*. New York: Knopf.

Rathmann, P. (1995). *Officer Buckle and Gloria*. New York: Putnam.

Modified Anticipation Guide

Donna J. Merkley

Volume 50, Number 4, December 1996/January 1997

Considerable research has established that a reader's comprehension is greatly influenced by his/her available background experiences (Pearson & Johnson, 1978; Pearson & Spiro, 1980; Taylor, 1979; Wilson & Hammill, 1982). If prior knowledge can be activated before reading and utilized during reading, comprehension is more complete (Baldwin, Peleg-Bruckner, & McClintock, 1985; Lipson, 1984; Pearson, Hansen, & Gordon, 1989).

An Anticipation Guide (AG) is a comprehension strategy designed to encourage interactive reading by requiring students to compare current beliefs and/or knowledge with text information. Typically, an AG consists of a series of statements in a forced response format. Students agree or disagree with each statement before reading, sharing reasons for their responses during a prereading discussion. This activity elicits students' thinking, arouses curiosity, and focuses attention. As they read, students encounter information that either

- verifies previously shared beliefs/ knowledge, or
- encourages alteration of the beliefs/ knowledge, or
- encourages comparison/contrast of beliefs and the new information.

After reading, students reconsider their initial responses with regard to the information that they encountered.

Numerous sources provide directions for AG construction and implementation (Duffelmeyer, 1994; Duffelmeyer, Baum, & Merkley, 1987; Ericson, Hubler, Bean, Smith, & McKenzie, 1987; Herber, 1978; Readence, Bean, & Baldwin, 1981; Richardson & Morgan, 1994). This article presents a modification of the traditional AG format that includes a prereading "I'm Not Sure" response option as well as differentiates the purpose for reading given to students.

Modification: Purpose for reading and "I'm Not Sure" option

Undergraduate tutors in our University Reading Improvement Clinic found the traditional AG response format (Agree/Disagree) to be appropriate when the statements were crafted to draw upon a reader's attitudes and/or opinions. Under these circumstances, tutors posed a purpose for reading that did not challenge the reader to consider changing his/her prereading attitudes or beliefs. Rather, the purpose for reading led the reader to compare his/her prereading responses to the responses a character from the selection or the author of the selection would make (see Figure 1, Part A).

Note both the nature of the statements and the purpose for reading in Figure 1. A fifth-grade reader typically has adequate experiences to formulate and explain prereading opinions concerning reasons for a move, being welcomed, and

---

Figure 1
AG for fifth grader studying early U.S. colonization

Part A

Prereading directions: Carefully read statements 1–4. Under the "You" heading, put a check (✔) in the Agree column if you mostly agree. Put a check (✔) in the Disagree column if you mostly disagree. Be ready to explain why you checked as you did.

You

Agree   Disagree

1. The main reason people move to a new location is for better paying jobs.
2. Strangers to an area are welcomed by people already living in that area.
3. Available transportation is a major concern when choosing a new place to live.
4. If given enough time, a new location always turns out to be a better place to live than the old location.

(Group and/or class discussion)

Part B

Purpose for reading: Now read pages 117–121 about immigration to the New World from England in the 1600s. When you finish p. 121, mark under the "Colonist" heading how you think a colonist would respond to each statement. Be sure to have proof from the text, pp. 117–121, to support why you think the colonist would agree or disagree.

Colonist

Agree   Disagree

1. The main reason people move to a new location is for better paying jobs.
2. Strangers to an area are welcomed by people already living in that area.
3. Available transportation is a major concern when choosing a new place to live.
4. If given enough time, a new location always turns out to be a better place to live than the old location.

(Group and/or class discussion)

the success of relocating. These experiences are activated as the reader shares his/her reasons to "Agree" or "Disagree." Because a single reading selection may not be powerful enough to change the reader's prereading opinion, the purpose for reading in Figure 1, Part B is for the reader to respond from another point of view. Citing proof from the selection, the reader can discuss how a colonist might respond to each statement. The tutor can then lead the reader to compare his/her prereading opinions and reasons to a postreading interpretation of the colonist's opinions and reasons.

When AG statements are created for factual selections, assessing the reader's prior knowledge of a topic rather than attitudes toward a topic is a typical goal. If the reader possesses incomplete background knowledge, the prereading forced response, Agree/Disagree, is often unproductive. The reader's prereading rationale for agreeing or disagreeing is understandably vague, ill defined, or inaccurate. Adding a prereading "I'm Not Sure" option tends to reduce blind guessing and offers insight into the reader's self-evaluation of his/her experiences with regard to the concepts under study (see Figure 2). Note that "I'm Not Sure" is not a postreading option.

This refinement addresses Lipson's (1984) concerns about the quality and quantity of a reader's prior knowledge. When Lipson examined the acquisition of new information with regard to children's ability to correct old but erroneous information, she found that "children were more likely to answer correctly on the posttest if they had marked an item 'unknown' on the pretest rather than given a wrong answer" (p. 761). Lipson found that children were more apt to attend to the textual information when they felt they did not already know the answer.

Therefore, when creating and implementing an AG for factual material, tutors need to be especially sensitive that the purpose for reading is to guide the reader in checking prior knowledge against concepts presented in the text. In the AG created for a factual piece entitled "The Why of Whiskers" (see Figure 2), the reading purpose "Read to see if you want to change any answers" directs the reader to determine if the text material is compatible with what he/she had asserted in the prereading exercise.

As a valuable prereading strategy the AG elicits students' thinking, arouses curiosity, focuses attention, and provides a basis for discussion. The modification suggested here offers further refinement to the teacher or tutor using this strategy.

REFERENCES

Baldwin, R.S., Peleg-Bruckner, Z., & McClintock, A.H. (1985). Effects of topic interest and prior knowledge on reading comprehension. *Reading Research Quarterly, 20,* 497–504.

Duffelmeyer, F.A. (1994). Effective anticipation guide statements for learning from expository prose. *Journal of Reading, 37,* 452–457.

Duffelmeyer, F.A., Baum, D., & Merkley, D.J. (1987). Maximizing reader-text confrontation with an extended anticipation guide. *Journal of Reading, 31,* 146–150.

Ericson, B., Hubler, M., Bean, T., Smith, C.C., & McKenzie, J.V. (1987). Increasing critical

Figure 2
AG for "The Why of Whiskers"

Part A

Prereading: Read each statement. Put a check (✔) in the "Agree" column if you agree. Put a check (✔) in the "Disagree" column if you disagree. Be ready to explain why you agree or disagree. If you are not sure, put a check (✔) in the "I'm Not Sure" column.

Agree   Disagree   I'm Not Sure

                        Whiskers are most useful to animals during the day.
                        Whiskers help animals hunt.
                        Some animals that have whiskers don't use them.
                        Wet whiskers aren't as useful as dry whiskers.

(Group/class discussion of responses and rationale)

Part B

Purpose for reading: Now read "The Why of Whiskers" to see if you want to change any of your answers. Notice that you can no longer say "I'm Not Sure," and remember to find support in the article for each of your answers.

Agree   Disagree

                        Whiskers are most useful to animals during the day.
                        Whiskers help animals hunt.
                        Some animals that have whiskers don't use them.
                        Wet whiskers aren't as useful as dry whiskers.

(Group/class discussion of responses and rationale)

The Why of Whiskers

Why do cats and other animals have whiskers? To help them know what's going on around them. Whiskers are organs of touch. Scientists call whiskers vibrissae (vi-BRIS-see). These long, straight hairs grow out of tiny pits in the skin. Around the roots of the hairs are very sensitive nerves. When an animal's whiskers feel something, these nerves tell the creature what it is.

Animals such as rabbits, deer, and wolves don't seem to rely on their whiskers. That's because these creatures are most active during the day. They use their sight and hearing to find food and enemies. Whiskers are most helpful to animals that usually prowl about in dark places. But scientists still don't know just how much these animals depend on their "feelers."

A cat's whiskers act just like tiny fingers when the animal hunts at night. They help the cat feel its way in the dark and keep it from bumping into things. When a cat sticks its head into a dark hole or tries to slip through a picket fence, its whiskers tell it how much room it has.

Whiskers also help some animals find food. A walrus, for example, has hundreds of thick, quill-like whiskers on its upper lip. In the deep, dark waters where it dives for clams, its sensitive whiskers feel for tasty treats in the mud.

Some seals and otters find food with their vibrissae, too. But many scientists say their whiskers act just like sonar! These animals hunt in waters where it's too dark or cloudy to see. Their whiskers can tell if a fish is moving up ahead and exactly where to find it.

Animal whiskers really are wonderful!

reading in junior high classes. *Journal of Reading, 30*, 430–439.

Herber, H.L. (1978). *Teaching reading in content areas.* Englewood Cliffs, NJ: Prentice-Hall.

Lipson, M. (1984). Some unexpected issues in prior knowledge and comprehension. *The Reading Teacher, 37*, 760–764.

Pearson, P.D., Hansen, J., & Gordon, C. (1989). The effect of background knowledge on young children's comprehension of explicit and implicit information. *Journal of Reading Behavior, 11*, 201–209.

Pearson, P.D., & Johnson, D.D. (1978). *Teaching reading comprehension.* New York: Holt, Rinehart & Winston.

Pearson, P.D., & Spiro, R.J. (1980). Toward a theory of reading comprehension instruction. *Topics of Language Disorder, 1*, 71–88.

Readence, J.E., Bean, T.W., & Baldwin, R.S. (1981). *Content area reading: An integrated approach.* Dubuque, IA: Kendall/Hunt.

Richardson, J.S., & Morgan, R.F. (1994). *Reading to learn in the content areas* (2nd ed.). Belmont, CA: Wadsworth.

Taylor, B.M. (1979). Good and poor readers' recall of familiar and unfamiliar text. *Journal of Reading Behavior, 11*, 375–380.

Wilson, C.R., & Hammill, C. (1982). Inferencing and comprehension in ninth graders reading geography textbooks. *Journal of Reading, 25*, 424–427.

Circle of questions

Mary Beth Sampson
Michael R. Sampson
Wayne Linek

VOLUME 48, NUMBER 4, DECEMBER 1994/JANUARY 1995

Five readers were reading their fifth grade science text. The information they read was about lightning bugs, and every reader was reacting differently to the text. Sarah read just to finish the assignment—she was daydreaming about what she would do that evening. Carlos read with great excitement—he had caught the first lightning bugs of spring the night before and had released them into his room, falling asleep to their steady blinks. Paul read with fascination. This was new information to him since he had just moved from Alaska, where lightning bugs did not exist. Marinda quickly discovered something she didn't know about lightning bugs from the text and instantaneously moved from being a passive reader to a really involved one. Josh read as he always did, word by word with no real interest in the content.

The children's attitudes soon changed dramatically. When they finished the text, their teacher, Mrs. Tollison, moved them quickly into a new literacy strategy, *Circle of Questions* (Sampson, Allen, & Sampson, in press). Here's how it happened.

The five students sat together at a table. Five other groups of five were at tables spread throughout the room. Students drew straws to see who would function as timekeeper, reporter, recorder, encourager, and leader. Mrs. Tollison announced that the topic was lightning bugs and that the groups' assignment was to brainstorm questions about lightning bugs.

After 3 minutes, Mrs. Tollison called "time." She then drew a circle on the chalkboard and invited each group to share their questions. Mrs. Tollison wrote the questions around the circle as the students shared them (see Figure).

The questions were reviewed and examined to determine the categories that existed. Mrs. Tollison used colored chalk to designate items that belonged in specific categories. Each group then chose a category in which to become an expert. As they reread, they searched for answers to the questions in that particular category. The recorders wrote their answers and where they were found in the text, and the reporters shared the information with the class. The teacher then wrote the answers and their sources by the appropriate questions.

Discussions occurred concerning particular questions and answers and whether the text adequately addressed the concerns. If not, additional research might be needed. Through the process, students' questions were answered. And the answers came from the children as they shared what they knew about the subject and what they had learned from the text.

What about Sarah, Carlos, Paul, Marinda, and Josh? How did the circle of

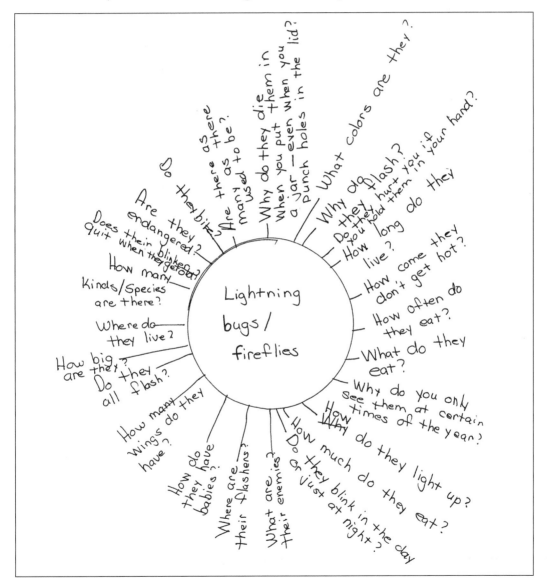

questions activity change these students in the group? Josh started to change his view toward reading that day. As his classmates generated questions they had about the text, he saw that all readers, not just himself, don't understand everything they read. Carlos gained valuable self-esteem that day because his knowledge of fireflies enabled him to answer many of the group's questions. Cooperative group skills were gained by all in the process of carrying out the various roles of time-keeper, recorder, reporter, encourager, and leader.

Circle of questions engages students in brainstorming, predicting, generating questions about text, categorizing, and interacting with text to answer those questions. As students use the strategy, they discover a valuable truth—the best way to clarify text is through group interaction with that text. Children become sharers of information as they fine-tune their spirit of inquiry.

As the students engage in this strategy, they begin to realize that not all questions are answered by a particular text, and sometimes more questions are raised. Even more importantly, they are actively constructing their own questions about a topic and then exploring the text to find answers—just as real readers do.

REFERENCE

Sampson, M., Allen, R.V., & Sampson, M.B. (in press). *Pathways to literacy: Process transactions*. Fort Worth, TX: Harcourt Brace.

Titling—Finding names that "mean"

Dorothy Grant Hennings
Gail McCreesh

VOLUME 48, NUMBER 2, OCTOBER 1994

An author puts a title on a story to entice readers and to communicate something about the story. S/he may choose a title that focuses on the setting (*The Haymeadow* by Paulsen), a character (*Stone Fox* by Gardiner), a feeling (*Missing May* by Rylant), an element of the plot (*Snow Treasure* by McSwigan), a symbol (*One More River* by Banks), or any key component of the story that s/he wishes to highlight. Similarly, an author focuses on these same dimensions of a story when creating titles for chapters.

Because titles are names that "mean," classroom teachers can use them to help children create their own meanings in response to what they read. Many teachers encourage children to use book and chapter titles to predict before reading. However, there are many other ways to use titles to involve students in story meanings.

Gail McCreesh encourages her third graders to analyze the titles for the chapters of a novel to see if there is a pattern, logic, or purpose to them. She asks students, "What do you think the author is trying to achieve with the chapter titles?" For example, in *Charlotte's Web* E.B.

White used titles to highlight time, characters, events, feelings, and places as shown in the titles to the first eight chapters: 1. Before Breakfast; 2. Wilbur; 3. Escape; 4. Loneliness; 5. Charlotte; 6. Summer Days; 7. Bad News; 8. A Talk at Home. In creating the titles, he varied the syntax, sometimes relying on a prepositional phrase to communicate time or place, sometimes using a noun to communicate character, events, or feelings. In contrast, John Gardiner used a noun pattern for the chapter titles in *Stone Fox* and named chapters after characters and key happenings from the story: 1. Grandfather; 2. Little Willy; 3. Searchlight; 4. The Reason; 5. The Way; 6. Stone Fox; 7. The Meeting; 8. The Day; 9. The Race; 10. The Finish Line. This is a pattern that third graders can easily understand. In both cases, the table of contents lists the titles, making analysis easier.

As her students read other chapter books in which authors have not titled chapters, Gail asks her third graders to *title in retrospect*—to create chapter titles after reading the book or a major segment of it. In titling in retrospect, students can use their understanding of an author's grand design and the meaning of a book as it touches their own lives. Working in collaborative groups, Gail's third-grade class created these titles to go along with the nine chapters of *Sarah, Plain and Tall* by Patricia MacLachlan: 1. Memories; 2. Letters from Sarah; 3. Our New Mother Sarah Is Coming; 4. Fun-loving Sarah; 5. A Perfect Dune for Us; 6. Sarah Learns About Winter; 7. Sarah and Maggie's Flower Garden; 8. The Big, Horrible Squall; 9. Caleb and Anna's Fears.

Gail sometimes suggests that students model their title making after the titles they have seen professional writers use. In creating titles, students at times play with parts-of-speech patterns as Gardiner did in *Stone Fox*. They name each chapter of a particular book with a proper noun, a determiner followed by a noun, an adjective followed by a noun, a prepositional phrase, a verb phrase, or with a kernel sentence. In the process, students refine their understanding of the way language works. Or they use their titles to focus on themes, moods, characters, or settings and, in the process, refine their understanding of story development.

Having worked cooperatively to name chapters of books they have read as a class, students do the same as they report on books they have read on their own: Rather than writing a typical book report, a student creates chapter titles that touch on significant meanings of a story.

With some books, Gail divides her class into teams based on the number of chapters (for example, nine teams if there are nine chapters). She assigns a chapter to each team. Without communicating with other teams, each team rereads the assigned chapter, cooperatively decides on a title that gets at the main idea, and records the title on a card. Gail then collects and distributes the cards to the groups in a random manner. Receiving a main idea card, each group decides the chapter to which it best applies, and they keep a record of the match. The groups switch cards and repeat the activity until all groups have tried to match all the titles with chapters. Gail has found this idea particularly useful with her third graders, who like to illustrate their title cards and organize them as a timeline to celebrate the chapter book they have just completed as a class. In upper grades, each team can create a main idea title for each chapter of a novel and put its titles in random order for another team to match, then share the reasoning behind their title choices and matches.

When an author has not broken a story into chapter segments (e.g., *Molly's Pilgrim* by Barbara Cohen), Gail has her third graders look for natural breaks that communicate changes in action, mood, or point of view. Talking together, they create titles to sum up each segment they have identified. In the same way, when uncaptioned illustrations complement a story, students add captions. Captions summarize story moods, actions, and/or characters. Again, student teams exchange their captions with other teams and match captions with illustrations. In the same way, students title the stanzas of poems and the acts and the scenes of plays they read or perform. This works at all grade levels, even with Shakespearean plays and narrative poems read in high school where again, students can exchange titles and try to match titles with scenes, acts, and stanzas. In doing this, students often begin to toy with the ultimate meaning of what they have read and the impact it has had on their own lives.

In using titling activities such as these, Gail has found that students enjoy the give and take of collaborative decision making. Working in teams, title-makers must weigh the pros and cons of various options. In doing this, they examine significant aspects of a story and arrive at a heightened understanding and appreciation of story meanings. These activities relate as well to writing. When youngsters title their own stories, they apply some of the same techniques that professional authors use. Students know that titles are not just words affixed to stories or chapters but are significant parts of stories; titles are names that "mean."

CHILDREN'S BOOKS CITED

Banks, L.R. (1992). *One more river*. New York: Morrow.

Cohen, B. (1983). *Molly's Pilgrim*. New York: Morrow.

Gardiner, J. (1980). *Stone Fox*. New York: Harper.

MacLachlan, P. (1985). *Sarah, plain and tall*. New York: Harper & Row.

McSwigan, M. (1942). *Snow treasure*. New York: Dutton.

Paulsen, G. (1992). *The haymeadow*. New York: Delacorte.

Rylant, C. (1992). *Missing May*. New York: Orchard.

White, E.B. (1952). *Charlotte's web*. New York: Harper & Row.

FINE

Susan Spear

VOLUME 47, NUMBER 1, SEPTEMBER 1993

Our multiage class of 8- through 10-year-olds was divided into small groups in order to prepare for our "trip" to the western region of the U.S. Students had their tickets in hand, maps at the ready, books, magazines, travel guides, and even some videotapes from which to begin their research. We had already decided to have an Exposition at the end of our trip, as we had done before. However, before we boarded the plane, we needed to talk as a whole group about how to assess our final project.

As the students recalled earlier projects, they began to brainstorm some of the things they thought were important to evaluate. While they talked I listed their suggestions on the board.

These were the ideas that we agreed were most important:

Facts—information that the students could build on in order to form ideas and concepts.

Interesting—information should be presented in such a way that it would be not only informative but also interesting to hear or view.

Neatness—important for overall appeal, reader response, and ease in gaining knowledge.

Effort—in small group situations, one student has the potential for letting the whole group down.

Having put these ideas on the board, we stopped for a moment to reflect on our thinking. Suddenly, one of the students cried out, "Look what the first letters make!"

And thus, FINE was born.

From that day on the students were able to look at almost any piece of work, written, drawn, built, or spoken, and decide quickly and easily if it was up to our FINE criteria or if it was NOT (*Not Our Thing*).

Alice in computerland: Using the Internet as a resource for teaching reading

Mary Jo Fresch

Volume 52, Number 6, March 1999

Alice was beginning to get very tired of sitting by her sister on the bank and of having nothing to do: once or twice she had peeped into the book her sister was reading, but it had no pictures or conversations in it, "and what is the use of a book," thought Alice, "without pictures or conversations?" (Carroll, 1968, p. 11)

Alice found her sister's pictureless book uninteresting. Perhaps she would enjoy her new electronic look—the online version of *Alice's Adventures in Wonderland* (http://www.megabrands.com/alice/alice.html). Lots of conversation, colorful pictures, and a Cheshire Cat that "winks" in and out of the tree branches. If Alice desires a language change, she can read her story in Italian—all available online.

Teachers are using resources available via computer in a number of ways. A recent survey of current use of computers dispelled several "myth(s) that computers and networks are just for math and the sciences" (Peha, 1995, p. 20). Kindergarten through Grade 12 teachers employed computers in all subject areas—31% of the time in science, 18% in social studies, 15% as a library aid, 15% in writing, 9% in foreign language, 6% in math, and 6% for other uses. This finding suggests that reading online can be incorporated in every area of the curriculum. Science reading could take place at *The Nine Planets* (http://seds.1pl.arizona.edu/billa/tnp) where the "history, mythology and current scientific knowledge of each of the planets and moons in our solar system" are available. Reading diaries of people who lived through a particular time in history can provide insights for children. A study of the U.S. Civil War might include The American Civil War Homepage (http://sunsite.utk.edu/civil-war/) where soldiers' diaries are available. Imagine small cooperative groups at Concertina Books—a Canadian publisher "committed to bringing books simultaneously to print and to the electronic highway" (http://www.iatech.com/books/intro.htm). Reading together, children can enjoy the graphics, storyline, and interactive nature of the text *Waking in Jerusalem* by Sharon Katz. The pages are colorful, and readers can quickly move through the text or stop and enjoy the sounds of birds and dogs. These small communities of learners have relied on the social nature of literacy learning as they explored print on the computer.

Not all sites are created equal. Some texts may appear as black print on a gray background. At first glance these seem rather boring. Yet even the simple texts have many possible classroom uses. For example, all the Grimm fairy tales are available online (gopher://world.std.com:70/11/obi/book/Fairy.Tales/Grimm/). By saving the text to your desktop hard drive or a disk, a number of reading activities can be devised. The text can be printed out (enlarging the type to the desired size) and cut apart for children to sequence.

The story is read aloud, and children work in small groups for the sequencing activity. Each group reads aloud the order of their story, and a discussion helps children discover what in the text allows us to understand the sequence of events. The same activity can be done without reading the story aloud before sequencing. The children share their version and talk about why they ordered segments as they did. Take the same text and replace some meaning-bearing words with blanks and you have a cloze activity. In the following example, from the Grimm Fairy Tale site, part of "The Elves and the Shoemaker" is shown as a cloze activity:

Once upon a time, there lived a _____ shoemaker. He lived in misery because as he grew_____ he could not see all that well anymore and he could not_____like he used to. One _____he went to bed sad, without finishing a repair job he had_____. In the _____he found the job done.

Internet versions of fairy tales can be compared to literature versions. Charts or Venn diagrams can compare and contrast story elements.

Plays provide another opportunity to practice reading. A text with speaking parts can be created by moving character names around in a play format. What was originally story text in the following Grimm tale was changed to a script by taking such lines as "said Mama Bear" and modifying the paragraph to be a speaking part:

Narrator 1: And in next to no time, Goldilocks lay fast asleep in Baby Bear's bed. In the meantime, the Bears were on their way home.

Baby Bear: Wasn't the new Beaver baby ever so small? Was I as tiny as that when I was born?

Mother Bear: Not quite, but almost.

Father Bear: (notices the door is ajar) Hurry! Someone is in our house...(looks at bowls) I knew it! Somebody has gobbled up the pudding....

Mother Bear: Someone has been jumping up and down on my armchair!

Baby Bear: ...and somebody's broken my chair!

Narrator 2: Where could the culprit be?

The Internet is a current, constantly changing, and extremely malleable resource. Unlike textbooks, World Wide Web sites provide reading in the content areas that can keep up with new information on a daily basis. This can complement any area of study. At the same time, the computer can allow children to collaborate during reading. Technology provides opportunities to expand and explore resources that enhance experiences with printed text. While the computer screen can never replace the joy of lap reading or go into the back seat of the car on our summer travels, it can be a wonderful addition to the world of reading.

Teachers interested in beginning their own journey through the Internet need a good search engine. Search engines hunt through sites, naming the ones that match a particular requested topic. Two favorites are Metacrawler (http://www.metacrawler.com) and Dogpile (http://www.dogpile.com/). These are multisearch engines that coordinate with several search engines. This saves time, because not all search engines will find what you are looking for. Another hint is to use a Boolean search, which makes your search a closed operation. That is, if reading comprehension is of interest, the search field should be typed as "reading + comprehension." This narrows the search to only sites that have both "reading" and "comprehension" related to them. If you are "curiouser and curiouser," start with some of these exciting literacy-related sites:

• Kathy Schrock's Guide for Educators has links to booktalks, lesson plans, writing guides, and much, much more (http://www.capecod.net/schrockguide/).

• The Los Angeles County Office of Education has organized some wonderful reading and writing links (http://teams.lacoe.edu./documentation/places/language.html).

• ERIC sites—all the various clearinghouses, including AskERIC, which contains lesson plans, infoguides, and helpful resources (http://www.aspensys.com/eric/sites/barak.html).

• Needle in a Cyberstack (http://home.revealed.net) is a wonderful "infofinder." One section links to all areas of the curriculum (http://home.revealed.net/~albee/pages/Curriculum.html).

• A document you can download and print out for parents is found in "Helping Your Child Learn to Read" from the Department of Education, written by Bea Cullinan and Brod Bagert (http://www.ed.gov/pubs/parents/Reading/).

• Tips, guides, and helpful resources from the University of Oregon are provided in the article "Learning to Read/Reading to Learn—Helping Children With Learning Disabilities to Succeed" (http://darkwing.uoregon.edu/~ncite/read.html).

• Pat Cunningham, Dorothy Hall, and

Margaret Defee help with planning your language arts block in their Four Blocks plan (http://www.wfu.edu/~ cunningh/fourblocks/).

• Get in touch with other educators at Web 66 International Registry of schools (http://web66.coled.umn.edu/schools.html).

• Finally, don't miss a valuable professional site—The International Reading Association (http://www.reading.org).

REFERENCES

Carroll, L. (1968). *Alice's adventures in Wonderland & Through the looking-glass.* New York: Magnum Books.

Peha, J.M. (1995). How K–12 teachers are using computer networks. *Educational Leadership, 53*(2).

The electronic journal: Combining literacy and technology

Jane Sullivan

VOLUME 52, NUMBER 1, SEPTEMBER 1998

A quiet coup has taken hold in language arts classrooms across the U.S. and with it have come welcome changes in the strategies we use to teach young learners reading and writing. Not the least of these innovations is the reflection teachers ask of their students as they read or write. "What meaning do you make of this text," today's teacher queries, "and how did you arrive at that conclusion?" Students respond—sometimes in writing, sometimes orally; sometimes alone, sometimes in concert with others. As communities of learners, they explore their literary worlds and share the results with their peers.

Much has been written in support of literature discussion groups (Gambrell & Almasi, 1996; Harwayne, 1992; Peterson & Eeds, 1990). In their description of a literature response project they conducted, Wollman-Bonilla and Werchadio (1995) report that despite the difference in length and quality of thought in the children's response journals, most of the entries let the teacher know whether the individual student understood the read-

ing. "There was no need for comprehension questions," the authors stated (p. 569).

There are additional benefits from such an approach. In *The Book Club Connection*, McMahon and Raphael (1997) remind their readers of the important role discussion plays in learning: "individuals construct a sense of self as they participate in social contexts; this identity includes their own and others' roles in the group" (p. 18).

Purpose of the project

Such radical changes in teaching demand a new approach in teacher education programs. University students in such preservice programs need opportunities to discuss literature, not only to develop classroom strategies for teaching literacy but also to discover for themselves the new insights one develops from shared inquiry about literature.

To promote such learning, I have for several years incorporated dialogue journal writing as an integral part of the reading methods course I teach. From its inception the required dialogue has involved interaction with elementary school students. Initially, the dialogues were handwritten journals carried back and forth between the university and school sites. However, with the introduction of classroom computers, the dialogue has taken on an electronic dimension. Students now use e-mail to hold their weekly "literature discussions." The particular project described here took place with 17 fifth- and sixth-grade special needs students at an elementary school in southern New Jersey. Twenty university students, enrolled in a reading methods course that focused on teaching such students, also took part.

For what purpose did we hold these discussions? In his book *To Think*, Frank Smith (1990) wrote, "Imagination is power. The creativeness of thought that enables us all to experience the world in which we live...makes it possible to construct new realities ourselves, and that is power indeed" (p. 32).

Working from Smith's premise that imagination is power, it is not difficult to hypothesize that discussing books that challenge the imagination would certainly empower both partners in the discussion—the preservice education student and the child in the classroom. And so, the primary purpose of this project was to stimulate the imagination of these children and their university partners, to guide them in the construction of new realities; that is, to empower them.

We can find further support for such a project in Harvey Daniels's book *Literature Circles* (1994), in which he describes such discussion groups in these words: "two potent ideas—independent reading and cooperative learning—come together in the elegant and exciting classroom activity called literature circles" (p. 12).

In this project, we expanded Daniels's model. My classroom teacher partner and I both believed that, by introducing e-mail into the model, we had added yet a third dimension—that of distance learning. We believed that, through distance learning, we would be able to accomplish the following three goals: (a) bring elementary school children and preservice teachers together, (b) discuss literature, and (c) integrate the language arts by weaving together activities that would involve reading, oral discussion, writing, and the use of technology.

Planning stage

My partner in this project was Chris, teacher of the special needs children with whom we worked. The computer specialist at the elementary school assisted in many ways, from acquiring e-mail addresses to instructing students on clipping and pasting their messages from a word processor to the e-mail site.

To launch our program there were certain things that I had to do with my students and certain preparations that Chris had to make. Chris and I, together with the computer specialist, met early in the semester in a planning session. At that meeting, we set up a strategy that would motivate students to engage in discussions.

I felt that my university students would gain from this experience in two ways. First, they would experience for themselves the approach students with difficulty in reading usually take when asked to respond to a passage—that of simply retelling the story. Second, they would be able to apply strategies we would discuss in class for getting students to go beyond that retelling. Chris, too, had positive expectations. In addition to the benefits from the strategies the university students would be applying, she felt that the project would motivate her students to do more independent reading.

Preparation of university students

In preparation for the project, I scheduled class time to teach my students the computer skills they might lack to allow them to use e-mail. Although all students enrolled in classes at the university are automatically assigned e-mail addresses, some had never accessed e-mail. Others, already familiar with e-mail, still needed to learn how to set up distribution lists, a time-saving strategy. And, like so many of us, all the students needed to learn how to stretch their patience to cover the many frustrations they were bound to encounter when entering the not-so-perfect world of technology. We also needed to discuss strategies that could be used to encourage students to move into in-depth reflections on the stories they read.

To carry out these preliminaries, I had my students form e-mail discussion circle groups. Using electronic mail, they formed groups of three or four and discussed one of two books: *Journey* by Patricia MacLachlan (1991) or *The Great Gilly Hopkins* by Katherine Paterson (1978). In those discussions, students were to focus on factors that would require higher level thinking strategies (e.g., interpretation, analysis, synthesis, value judgments). In their responses they were to react to one or more of the following topics: (a) character development, (b) literary devices, (c) relationship to personal experiences, and (d) theme of the selection.

Students did just that. For example, Jim linked the story in *Journey* to his own life when he wrote, "I enjoyed the book because it reminded me a great deal of my own grandparents....At any event throughout my life, the camera was aways there right along with my grandfather. Before reading *Journey*, I never really gave much thought to the significance of his camera in his life."

Kathy shared a response from an aesthetic stance in an entry she wrote about *The Great Gilly Hopkins*: "I didn't like the way *TGGH* ended. I wanted Gilly to go back to Mrs. Trotter. When I read a book, I want a happy ending. Gilly may have been happy to find her family, but I thought she would have been happier with Mrs. Trotter."

And in response to the same book, Gloria wrote, "I found Gilly very similar to the children I work with. They put you through their own personal training, and when you pass with flying colors (if you do), they will love you forever." This entry revealed to us that Gilly was not a stranger to this student, but rather an example of that "new reality" of which Frank Smith speaks, the reality that emerges from the imagination and empowers us.

My students were able to exchange four messages while waiting for Chris to prepare her students. By then I felt that they had grasped the purpose for the project and were ready to exchange messages with the elementary school students.

Just before we began the exchange between the elementary school students and the university students, I gave my students a final preproject assignment. Chris had selected four books that we would use for the discussions:

(a) *The Bears' House*, Marilyn Sachs (1971),

(b) *The Pinballs*, Betsy Byars (1977),

(c) *The Fighting Ground*, Avi (1984), and

(d) *Jacob Have I Loved*, Katherine Paterson (1980).

There is a common theme running through each of these selections. I wanted my students, regardless of the book they were assigned, to address that theme. So I gave them this autobiographical assignment before they began reading their assigned book:

> In each of the books we will be reading with children, the main character either misunderstood another character's intentions or was misunderstood her/himself. Write a paragraph to your e-mail partners. In it, recall an experience from your own life in which misunderstanding played a role.

Students wrote some surprisingly candid responses to this prompt. Some shared how they had misunderstood their university roommates until they got to know them better. Others shared misperceptions they had had of their parents. Most of the vignettes the students wrote were quite personal. I believe the activity set the stage for the reading and responding that was to follow.

Preparation of the elementary school students

While the university students were learning strategies to guide students' responses to reading, the elementary school students were also learning new tasks. In addition to learning to use e-mail, they were holding literature circle discussions and translating the ideas they got from that discussion into writing.

Chris had set up a sequence of steps in her class routine that would lead her students to the final task of sending their e-mail messages. They would first form discussion circles with their classmates who were reading the same book. During this Literature Circle time, they would share their responses to the part of the story that Chris had assigned for independent reading time. Also at that time, they would retrieve the messages that their university partners had sent.

Sometimes those messages would focus on the same portion of text Chris's students had discussed. At other times, because of the time lag between class sessions, the university students' responses added some information to the previous week's response.

Depending on the responses, each of the elementary school students would draft an appropriate return response on the word processor. Chris would review each draft to be certain that the message did indeed acknowledge the university students' messages and that it would focus on the reading, avoid tangential remarks, and move beyond a simple retelling of the story.

The students would receive Chris's comments on the following day and work on any necessary revisions. Satisfied that their messages were ready for publication, students clipped and pasted them onto the e-mail screen. Since the process took place over several days, the timing dovetailed nicely with the once-a-week meeting schedule of the university students.

The electronic mail discussions

As an official opening to the project, both Chris and I made videotapes of the students so that they could see who their e-mail partners were. We also put students into groups of four—two elementary school students and two university students, rather than in pairs. (The unevenly numbered classes made it necessary to form 3 three-member groups made up of one elementary student and two university students.) In this way, if one member of the group did not respond, chances were greater that there would still be at least one message waiting for a partner on either end.

A month and a half into the semester, the university/elementary school dialogue got off to a somewhat rocky start. Nonfunctioning e-mail addresses, typographical errors, and returned messages all contributed to a less than successful beginning. Nevertheless, the message exchange continued until the end of the university's semester.

What we found

Even preliminary examination of the responses indicated positive results. Students were interested in what their partners had to say. Their responses reflected a conversation, albeit in cyberspace. Jim, the university student (U), and Adam, the elementary school student (ES), for example, had this exchange:

Adam: I read that Jonathan was milking a cow. I think that was hard work. Have you ever milked a cow? I would want to.

Jim: Adam, you really seem to become involved in the story as you read. Your question about milking a cow brings me right into the story along with you and Jonathan. Yes, I have milked a cow and it is hard work. You must have very strong fingers and you press your head against the cow as you reach for the udder.

And, having finished the book, Adam made this perceptive comment about the conclusion of the story as well as on the logic (or illogic) of war:

I think he [Jonathan] was brave. When the war started, he was. Before, he always dreamed about it [the war], but now he thinks he's going to get killed. He wishes that he listened to his father. I don't like war. If everybody didn't want to go to war, there wouldn't be war.

Valerie (ES) and Lori (U) examined characters in *Jacob Have I Loved*. They shared this exchange:

Valerie: The two sisters in this story are not the I-love-my-sister-I-don't-know-what-I-will-ever-do-without-her type. Louise is always feeling that she is left out ever since she was a baby and her twin Caroline took the spotlight. Lori and Vanessa, do you ever have that you-don't-fit-in feeling?

Lori: I agree with what you said about the two sisters. I have had a couple of experiences where I have felt left out and unnoticed. When my sister and I were younger, my family would make a big deal about how well my sister could sing. I, on the other hand, was shy so I kept to myself a lot of the time. I felt a little left out because I thought my family thought my sister was better than me.... My sister is still more talkative...but I know that no matter what we are both loved equally.

Heather (ES) and Jill (U) had an exchange about the symbolism evidenced in *The Bears' House.*

Heather: I would like to ask you some questions. Who is Goldilocks to Fran? I think that she is a sister or a friend.

Jill: I believe Goldilocks was Fran Ellen's imaginary friend. This was a way Fran escaped from reality. This made her very happy. Sometimes, when you use your sense of imagination, it helps you get through some bumpy roads that are ahead of you.

It was evident that, as the project moved toward completion, the elementary school student responses became more specific. There was increasing evidence that they were focusing on character analysis and making connections between the story and real life. One week into the project, for example, one elementary school student wrote:

I am reading *Pinballs*. I think the characters talk too much. What do you think of the book so far?

But, after a month, that same student sent messages that evidenced a deepening reflection, such as:

I think Harvey's dad wants him back. Harvey and his dad went out to dinner. They talked about Harvey's mother.

and

Thomas J. is getting along with Mr. Mason. Have you ever visited anybody in the hospital and then become frightened?

Both university and elementary school students reported the experience as a positive one. Ann's (U) assessment is typical of those I received from my students. She wrote:

Discussing literature with peers affords the opportunity for us, as teachers, to gain new strategies. E-mail also brings teachable moments.... When the child raises an issue, you can give the child a different outlook or a deeper understanding....

The elementary students' incentive to read appeared to increase. Parents of Chris's students told her that their children were reading independently without being coaxed. And one elementary student reported to me in a message that she found herself reading more carefully because "I knew that I was going to write about what I was reading." Chris also felt that the experience of "reading a book from cover to cover" as opposed to the literature anthology that was their usual fare motivated students. Perhaps the closure they experienced at the end of the reading, that feeling of "Hey, I just read a book on my own," awakened a new interest in reading as well as a sense of achievement.

I think the best evidence that the project had proven to be worthwhile was that, despite the delays, the bugs, the returned messages, and the unavoidable frustrations with technology, the university students wanted to continue the discussion, and Chris invited me to do it again next year.

REFERENCES

Daniels, H. (1994). *Literature circles: Voice and choice in the student-centered classroom.* York, ME: Stenhouse.

Gambrell, L., & Almasi, J. (Eds.). (1996). *Lively discussions: Fostering engaged reading.* Newark, DE: International Reading Association.

Harwayne, S. (1992). *Lasting impressions: Weaving literature into the writing workshop.* Portsmouth, NH: Heinemann.

McMahon, S., & Raphael, T. (1997). The book club program: Theoretical and research foundations. In S. McMahon, T. Raphael, V. Goatley, & L. Pardo (Eds.), *The book club connection.* New York: Teachers College Press.

Peterson, R., & Eeds, M. (1990). *Grand conversations.* New York: Scholastic.

Smith, F. (1990). *To think.* New York: Teachers College Press.

Wollman-Bonilla, J., & Werchadio, B. (1995). Literature response journals in a first-grade classroom. *Language Arts, 72,* 562–570.

CHILDREN'S BOOKS CITED

Avi. (1984). *The fighting ground.* New York: HarperCollins.

Byars, B. (1977). *The pinballs.* New York: HarperCollins.

MacLachlan, P. (1991). *Journey.* New York: Bantam Doubleday Dell.

Paterson, K. (1978). *The great Gilly Hopkins.* New York: HarperCollins.

Paterson, K. (1980). *Jacob have I loved.* New York: HarperCollins.

Sachs, M. (1971). *The bears' house.* New York: Puffin.

Stuco-Slides enhance literacy and content learning

Cindy Wilson

VOLUME 50, NUMBER 4, DECEMBER 1996/JANUARY 1997

One of my favorite techniques to use with students from kindergarten through high school is student-constructed photographic slides. Slide construction is an adventure that can "cement" or "paste" learning together for students, and this consequently led me to the name Stuco-Slides (pronounced stuc'o) for *student* constructed slides.

Slide construction is fun and exciting and offers many literacy rewards for students and teachers. Through slide construction and slide show presentation students practice brainstorming and planning, problem solving, reading, writing, thinking, and sharing. Often art, music, listening, speaking, and research also play an integral role. As learners design and construct their own slides, they respond to information available to them, often seeking new knowledge and then tying these concepts to their prior knowledge. In an attempt to showcase their ideas and understanding, the empowered learners build a visual (and sometimes auditorially supported) display.

I have used Stuco-Slides with primary grades in story retellings, in intermediate grades and middle school for literature response activities, and in high school for project presentations. These simple student- or teacher-created slides have been used for developing background knowledge, setting purpose, reinforcing vocabulary, stimulating interest, and motivation. Stuco-Slides can even be used for assessment and evaluation. My sixth graders thought that test-taking was "cool" when presented in the form of a slide show!

Stuco-Slides are easy for students and teachers to make. Once the teacher has modeled the process, the class should be guided through the development of a slide show. These basic steps can be posted in the room as instructions:

Step 1: Create a grid. Teachers may prefer to make the classroom grid themselves to save time. If made on white posterboard, this grid may be used over and over. Using a black marker and T-square, draw the grid outline. The grid must be a 16" × 21" rectangle divided into 24 equal sections with four columns down and six rows across (see Figure 1).

Figure 1
The Stuco-Slide grid

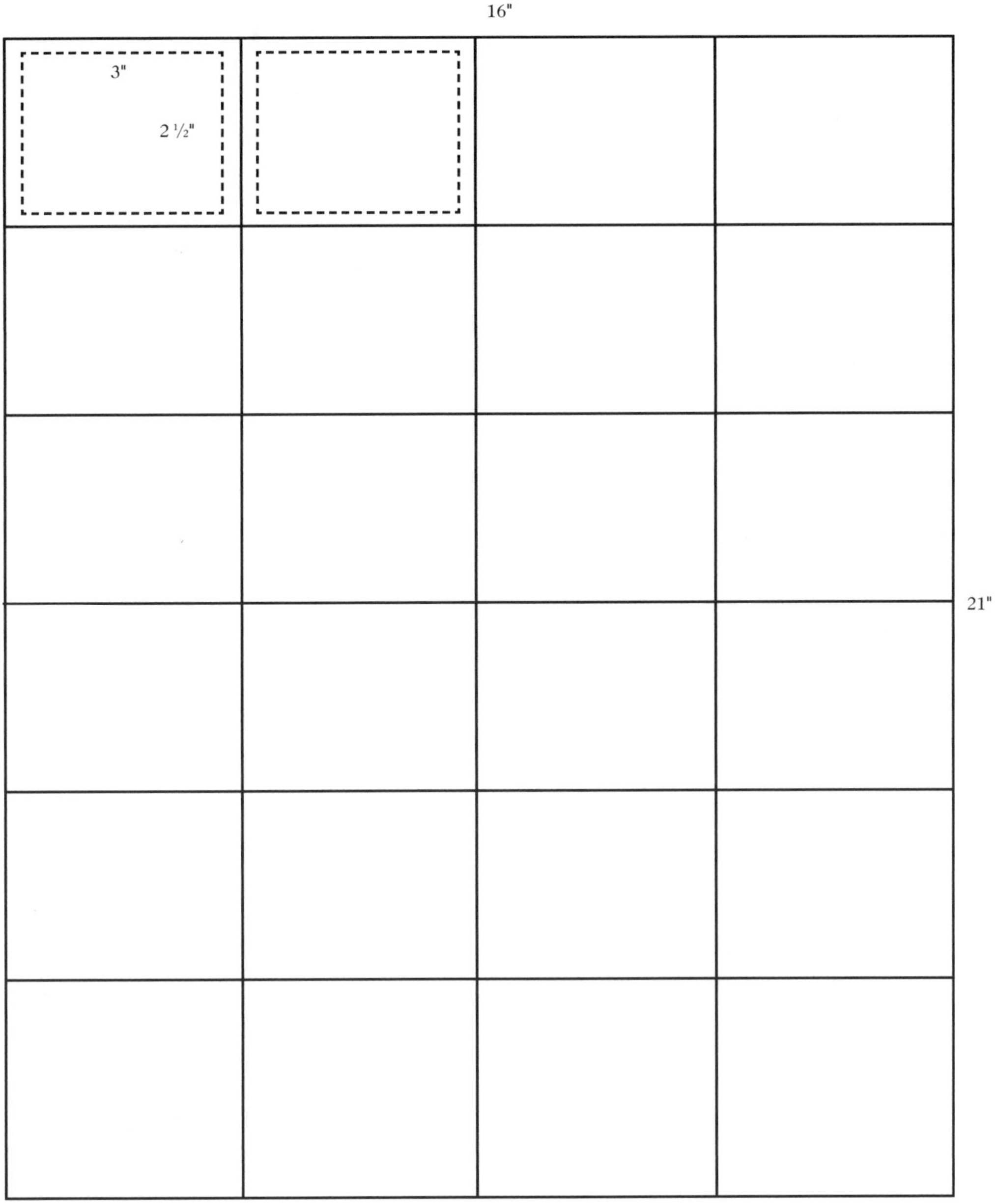

16"

3"

2 ½"

21"

Step 2: Cut squares of white paper 3" × 2½", which are the templates for the actual slides. Students write, draw, diagram, design, type, or interpret in visual form what they want their slide to look like. Black or red felt-tip pens work best. Since black and red become negative on the slide, instruct students that whatever they outline or fill in will be clear on the slide (see Figure 2).

Step 3: Rubber cement the paper slip to the grid. A grid will make 24 slides at one time. If you do not use all of the squares on the grid at one time, try gluing a 3" × 2½" slip of black paper in the remaining areas. These make wonderful empty slides for later use. Using rubber cement allows you to pull off the old slips and place new ones on for repeated use.

Step 4: Take the entire grid to an offset printer in your school system or town. Have the printer make a negative of your grid by reducing it to a 38% setting. The result will be a negative about the size of a piece of typing paper.

Step 5: Cut the negative into individual slides along the clear grid lines.

Step 6: Using colored markers, fill in the clear areas of each negative with desired hues. Colors will last longer if students color the dull side of the negative. Do not worry about staying in the lines—color overlapping the black will not show.

Step 7: Place the negative into a slide sleeve. These can be purchased at any camera shop and may be used over and

Figure 2
Stuco-Slide negative

over. If the slide does not quite center, use a small piece of clear tape to secure it.

Step 8: Arrange your slides and have a show! You may want to number the slides in order for future reference or in case they are spilled.

Once students become familiar with making slides and feel comfortable creating them, the supplies may be set up in the writing center for learners to use at any time. Giving students the opportunity to explore reading and writing on any topic of study through constructing slides is beneficial for everyone. Students are empowered to use reading, writing, listening, speaking, and thinking skills to make visual representations of their learning. Success and pride result from purposeful and powerful learning activities like Stuco-Slides. Good luck in your productions!

Picturing story: An irresistible pathway into literacy

Beth Olshansky

Volume 50, Number 7, April 1997

Unlike traditional approaches to literacy learning, Image-Making Within the Writing Process, an interactive program created at the University of New Hampshire, begins with the irresistible invitation to "mess with paints." The U.S. Department of Education has called the literacy program innovative and effective; the colorful art-based literacy program is designed to entice even the most discouraged of learners.

Image-Making begins with a series of process-oriented art explorations. The first step, creating individual portfolios of hand-painted, textured papers, never fails to captivate all those involved. As children fill paper after paper with bright colors and unusual textures, they delight in their beautiful paintings. The only instructions the teacher gives are to "fill each page with color and texture" and to avoid making representational images; every child experiences immediate success as an artist.

After this initial flurry of excitement over the paper-texturing experience, the children are given time to admire their hand-painted, textured papers, share them with one another, and discover images in their creations. As children engage in this process of discovery through free association, their abstract paintings serve as the inspiration for story ideas. As stories begin to surface, the beautiful, textured papers become the raw materials for cutting and pasting collage images.

Angeline, a third-grade student and second-language learner, wrote about her process, "I looked at the images in my prints. I saw so many flowers. Then I said, I will name my story 'The Beautiful Garden and the Rain.' I cut some pictures out, and I just glued and glued until it was so beautiful." After creating collage images, Angeline went on to orally rehearse and then finally write out her text. Angeline confessed, "And I even hated to read before." With pride, she added, "Now I love reading and making stories!"

Concrete tools

Image-Making offers children concrete tools for thinking through and designing stories. As children discover stories in their beautiful, textured papers and then cut and paste colorful collage images, they are literally giving shape to their ideas. While the children delight in the stunning visuals they create, they use visual and kinesthetic modes of thinking as they create a story. Children who struggle with straight verbal methods have an opportunity to work from their strengths. For some, this can mean the difference between success and failure in literacy learning.

David, a discouraged second grader, is one of those students. After refusing to write for the first 2 months of school, David explained to his teacher, "I hate to write. The words fly out of my head before I can get them down on paper." But things changed for David when he discovered that as he gave shape to his ideas through cutting and pasting, his story ideas were literally glued to the page. His thoughts no longer escaped him. With his concrete story map in hand, David was free to rehearse and develop his text, repeating it over and over again until at last he memorized his story line. From there, it was simple to put his colorful ideas into writing.

This hands-on story design and oral rehearsal of text offer children who struggle with straight verbal methods a way to succeed. Today, David is a professionally published author/illustrator. His second-grade story, *The Horrified Tornado*, is one of many stories that have been pub-lished in order to share this rich process with others.

A universal approach

Picturing a story using collages made from hand-painted, textured papers paves the way for children to interact with print in a highly personal, meaningful, and engaging way. As an alternative to verbal means of teaching reading and writing, Image-Making provides an enticing pathway into literacy for children with a wide range of learning needs. For children, never before has writing been made so easy and so much fun. No longer do they have to stare at a blank piece of lined paper and wonder what to write about or have to write on assigned topics that hold little interest. Through the process of free association, cutting, pasting, and manipulating paper, personal stories pour forth from the children in vivid color.

As educators learn more about the importance of honoring learning styles, tapping into multiple intelligences, using whole-brain thinking, and structuring tasks that are developmentally appropriate, Image-Making is an approach to literacy learning that makes sense for children everywhere. Not only does it capture the fancy of young writers and provide them with new tools for thinking, it also offers children a universal means of expression. For second-language learners as well as for other children who struggle with written language, Image-Making provides an irresistible pathway into literacy.

Author's note

The Horrified Tornado and six other titles written and illustrated by children are available by writing to Image-Making Within the Writing Process, Laboratory for Interactive Learning, University of New Hampshire, Thompson Hall, 105 Main Street, Durham, NH 03824, USA.

Language arts:
A success story

Mitzi Minnick Hook
Joyce Kirkpatrick

VOLUME 48, NUMBER 1, SEPTEMBER 1994

Mitzi's turn:

I was in the midst of a language arts unit on folktales and needed some additional titles to spark student interest. So I went to the media center to supplement the text. Keeping in mind the varied background of my class, I purposely searched for materials from other cultures. I found a wonderful book, *Iktomi and the Berries* by Paul Goble (1989), who has authored many other Native American stories. What intrigued me most about his stories of Iktomi was the modern day point of view. Also, the book was funny and I knew that would appeal to my students.

Instead of just having students read additional folktales, I decided to have them retell a tale of their choice. My purpose was to hone their oral communication skills and to further expose them to real literature.

At this point, I involved our school media specialist in this project.

Joyce's turn:

When Mitzi approached me with her folktale dilemma, I was not exactly sure how I could help. But as we talked, it became clear that I could do one of my favorite things for her class...storytelling! When the children arrived, I was in costume and told *The Talking Eggs* by Robert San Souci (1989), one of my favorites. I did not divulge my true identity, so they went away guessing until the next session.

Mitzi's turn:

I contacted a professional storyteller and arranged for him to visit our classroom. He shared three stories from his repertoire. After hearing both storytellers, students brainstormed the characteristics of good storytelling.

Joyce's turn:

When Mitzi's class came back to see me, I shared my entire bag of tricks. First I showed them my "Talking Eggs" costume: a grey wig (with bun), a shawl, some granny glasses, and a fake egg (total costume cost—US$3.50).

I shared my story apron with them; it is a plain muslin, pocketed apron with velcro attached at the top. I drew scenery with markers on squares of sheeting material, using the velcro to change the setting of my story. Hand puppets pulled from the pockets acted out *The Funny Little Woman* by Arlene Mosel (1972) (cost—$2.50).

Shadow puppets, used on the overhead projector, are easily and cheaply made from paper and florist wire. I acted out *The Little Old Lady Who Was Not Afraid of Anything* by Linda Williams (1986) with these simple cutouts.

I am a real collector and have a huge cache of hats. Using them made telling *The Three Hat Day* by Laura Geringer (1985) so much fun. There are many other hat books which can be extended, such as *Jennie's Hat* by Ezra Jack Keats (1966) and *Maebelle's Suitcase* by Trisha Tusa (1987).

Many props can be found around the house. *Jim and the Beanstalk* by Raymond Briggs (1970) is made "bigger" by forming giant eyeglasses out of coathangers, enormous coins of poster board covered with gold wrapping paper, and a giant wig out of fake fur remnant. In addition, I encouraged my daughter, the skee ball freak, to select a huge comb as her prize. I have developed an eye for junk that can be used to make a story come alive. I urged Mitzi's students to enlist their parents' help in exploring the house to locate good props.

Students were also given the option of borrowing some commercially prepared transparencies available in our media center. Each transparency, when shown on a wall, becomes scenery for a wide variety of folktales, fairy tales, and legends.

Before the class left, I mentioned some tips for storytelling success. To learn stories, I audiotape myself and listen over and over to get the story line and voice inflection just right. Sometimes I videotape myself or practice in front of a mirror to become comfortable with gestures and manipulating props or puppets. Adopting a dialect or special voice is appropriate if it can be maintained throughout the entire telling. We talked about the importance of eye contact and choosing a story with a simple plot and few characters. We also talked about the importance of selecting a story that the storyteller really likes. I told the students that it's OK to drop a story if you discover it's not working out as you planned. I encouraged them to seek my help if problems occurred.

Mitzi's turn:

Because of the nature of this assignment, we needed an alternative means of assessment. I asked students to verbalize what makes them listen. As a followup to our previous discussion about what makes a successful storyteller, we listed the criteria and assigned point values for each. following is the rubric my class designed:

Storyteller's name:_____

Oral communication

Purpose: Retell a folktale, legend, or fairy tale

Criteria: 1 = weak
             2 = average
             3 = good

I. Storytelling

Expression	1	2	3
Use of prop	1	2	3
Loudness	1	2	3
Enthusiasm	1	2	3
Eye contact	1	2	3
Preparation	1	2	3
Tells the story clearly	1	2	3

II. Listening skills

1 Impolite, inattentive behavior

2 Needs improvement in polite and attentive behavior

3 Polite, attentive behavior at all times

With the rubric in hand, students were better able to prepare for their performances.

Students used class time to practice in groups of three or four. They gave each other feedback in the form of suggestions for alternative prop usage and cues about volume or eye contact. Students who were dissatisfied with elements of their telling could then choose to make adjustments or change stories altogether. Part of the requirement was to practice at home so that they would feel more comfortable with an audience.

I arranged a special arena for performing. The storytelling area in our media center was available for us, but I would have created a suitable environment within my classroom if that had not been the case. It was important for the audience to be situated in a manner that lent itself to attentive listening.

After each story was told, the entire audience shared positive comments and constructive ideas for future tellings. Student interaction influenced my evalua-tions, making this process more worth-while. Students felt real pride and genuine ownership of their work.

Other teachers in the school heard of what we were doing and wanted my students to tell stories in their classes. I let volunteers go to the class of their choice to perform.

Joyce's turn:

I volunteered to tape each student in full costume and/or with props for the class video yearbook. Students helped superimpose their names using our video character generator.

I was amazed at the fantastic effort that Mitzi's class put into this unit of study. It was a real thrill for me to have been a part of this experience!

Mitzi's turn:

This spontaneous lesson developed into the highlight of my teaching career. I've never been more excited by the quality of work produced or my students' genuine enthusiasm. Ross continues to be held in high esteem as Wiley and the Hairy Man. Dorothy wrote an original folktale, which became a schoolwide winner in our county writing competition.

And the learning continues!

CHILDREN'S BOOKS

Briggs, R. (1970). *Jim and the beanstalk.* New York: Coward-McCann.

Geringer, L. (1985). *The three hat day.* New York: Harper and Row.

Goble, P. (1989). *Iktomi and the berries*. New York: Orchard.

Keats, E.J. (1966). *Jennie's hat*. New York: Harper and Row.

Mosel, A. (1972). *The funny little woman*. New York: Dutton.

San Souci, R. (1989). *The talking eggs*. New York: Dial.

Tusa, T. (1987). *Maebelle's suitcase*. New York: Macmillan.

Williams, L. (1986). *The little old lady who was not afraid of anything*. New York: Crowell.

From script to stage:
Tips for Readers Theatre

Aaron Shepard

VOLUME 48, NUMBER 2, OCTOBER 1994

Readers Theatre is often defined by what it is not—no memorizing, no props, no costumes, no sets. All this makes Readers Theatre wonderfully convenient. Still, convenience is not its chief asset. Like storytelling, Readers Theatre can create images by suggestion that could never be portrayed realistically on stage. Space and time can be shrunk or stretched, fantastic worlds can be created, marvelous journeys can be enacted. Readers Theatre frees the performers and the audience from the physical limitations of conventional theater, letting the imagination soar.

The style of Readers Theatre described in this article was developed by Chamber Readers, a nonprofit Readers Theatre company in Humboldt County, California, that has promoted reading and literature since 1975. Two teams, each with four readers, are directed by Jean Wagner, one of the founding members. Chamber Readers performs each year in nearly every public school in the county and is considered a local institution.

Like traditional Readers Theatre, the Chamber Readers' style is based on script reading and the suggestive power of language. But it adds a good deal of mime and movement as well. That's a bit more work, but it can be more fun too! (For the traditional approach, see Caroline Feller Bauer's *Presenting Reader's Theater: Plays and Poems to Read Aloud*, 1987, New York: H.W. Wilson. For tips on scripting, see the appendix to my collection *Stories on Stage: Scripts for Reader's Theater*, 1993, New York: H.W. Wilson.)

Briefly, the distinctive features of the Chamber Readers' approach are (a) characters move around the stage much as in a play, acting out or suggesting the movements described in the story, often by simple mime devices like walking in place; (b) though narrators look at the audience, characters most often look at each other; (c) scripts in sturdy binders are held in one hand, leaving the other hand free for gesturing; and (d) a set of low stools and a single high stool serve as versatile stage scenery or props.

Following is a detailed discussion of these and other elements. The word stage here means stage area, which could be the front of a classroom. An actual stage isn't needed.

Equipment

For Readers Theatre, you really need nothing but scripts, but a little basic equipment can add a lot. Here are some suggestions:

• Script binders. Sturdy ring binders are best. Whatever you use, make sure the pages turn easily. On stage, the binder may also become a prop, representing a book, a notepad, the surface of a table.

• Smocks. These give the readers a team look yet are also neutral, so readers can easily change character in the minds of the audience. The smock can be a simple rectangle of cloth with a head hole, fastened together at the sides.

• Stools of chair height. These are your most useful props. For some stories, you won't need any; for others, you may need one for each reader on stage. They must be solid enough to stand on!

• High stools. One or two should be enough. These too should be solid enough for standing.

• Portable screens. These are strictly optional, but they're fun to use if they're handy. They provide an alternative for entrances and exits and for some special effects.

• Small props. These can sometimes add nice touches—as when a Pied Piper has a tin whistle to play.

Script handling

The trick with scripts is to handle them so they can be referred to easily but don't seriously restrict movement or distract the audience. The script is held in one hand, leaving the other free for acting. For a relaxed grip, the binder spine can simply lie in the palm. If readers move around a lot, they can instead grip the binder's top edge. Part of the binder rests against the upturned forearm. Right-handers usually hold a script with their left hand, left-handers with their right.

Though readers don't need to memorize, they should know their lines and cues well enough so they can look up from their scripts about half the time. When they *do* look down, it's only with the eyes, keeping the head straight up. A character who has to look upward for much of a scene may have to memorize part of the script. A narrator who has a long speech may have to use a free hand to keep the place. A reader who will have no free hand when a page must be turned can place that page backward in the binder to get two pages facing.

The set

You don't construct sets for Readers Theatre, but you can *suggest* them. The narrator's descriptions are brought to life by the readers' movements and mime. If a reader opens a door, we see it. If readers hang ornaments on a Christmas tree, we know right where it is.

Stools are a chief aid for suggesting sets, as well as being practical props.

Three short stools in a semicircle can be a dining room. Two short stools close by each other can be a bench in a park, or a roof ridge atop a house. A single high stool can be a throne room. A high stool with a short stool next to it can be a tree to climb or a mountain. An area with no stools can be anything at all!

As in theater, you start designing your set by figuring out what locations your script calls for. Then you position those locations on your stage in whatever arrangement works and looks best. Look for ease of reader movement, stage balance, and openness to the audience.

Readers can move to different stage areas for different scenes. Or they can stay in the same area, and you can change the set. Or the set can move to them! For instance, a reader could move from room to room in a house just by walking in place, climbing some stairs, and opening some doors—all without moving an inch.

Reader movement

After designing your set, decide where your readers will start and where they will go. Drawing a series of movement diagrams can help you spot problems, save time during rehearsal, and jog your memory the next time you use the script. In one simple diagram system, circles are low stools, double circles are high stools, crosses are readers, and arrows show movement.

To go offstage, a reader doesn't actually need to leave the area but can instead go back to audience (BTA), which indicates that the reader is out of the picture.

If sitting on a stool, the reader can usually just turn around on it. If standing, the reader can move toward the back of the stage. Narrators seldom go BTA, even if they're not reading for awhile.

In regular theater, the curtain or the lights coming down indicates a scene change, a jump in time or place. In Readers Theatre, this change is shown by some kind of break in movement. For instance, the readers can all freeze in place like statues. Or they can turn BTA, freeze, then come back in. Or they can freeze, then cross the stage for the next scene. If one scene flows smoothly into the next, without a jump, you may not need a break at all.

Mime and sound effects

Whatever action is described in the script, readers should try either to do it or else to suggest it through mime. If someone is eating, we should see the fork carried to the mouth. If someone is hanging in the air, we should see the arm pulled tight by the floating balloon. If someone is racing a horse, we should see the galloping hooves.

The key word here is *suggest*, because the movements are often far from realistic. For instance, it's hard to take off a coat realistically when one hand holds a script. Readers quickly learn to sleep sitting up, with their heads bent to the side. And walking in place is a reader's favorite mode of travel.

Mime techniques add polish to a performance. It's always good to draw on proven tricks for walking in place, climbing up or down stairs or ropes or ladders, lifting or pulling heavy objects, flying, falling, and so on. Look for library books on mime or invite a local mime to conduct a workshop.

Part of successful group mime is being aware of the invisible. If a stool is meant to be a chair at a table, make sure no one walks through the table! Even a door that's invisible shouldn't shift position as different people pass through it. If two characters look at a picture on the wall, they will hopefully agree where it is!

Sounds in the story too should be added where possible—explosions, wind, bees, roosters, whatever. To help the illusion, this is usually handled by readers who are BTA.

Focus

Focus refers to where the readers are looking. Most of the time, it's simple: Narrators use *audience focus*—they look straight at the audience. Characters use *onstage focus*—they look at whoever they're talking to, just as in plays or real life.

But sometimes you may want characters to use *off-stage focus*. The readers imagine a screen facing them, as wide as the stage, set up at the front edge of the audience. On this screen they imagine a mirror image of all the readers. Then instead of talking straight to each other, they talk to each other's image. Off-stage focus can help create illusions of distance or height. Two characters on the same stage but using off-stage focus can shout and wave at each other as if a mile apart. If one looks upward and one looks downward, you have a midget talking to a giant, or a woman in a window talking to a man in the street.

Characters can, at times, address comments directly to the audience. They might also use this focus if the audience is drawn into the story, as might happen, for instance, if the audience suddenly becomes a hill completely covered with cats.

Beginnings and endings

Beginnings and endings should be rehearsed along with the story so they'll go smoothly. One reader should introduce the story with at least the title and author. Beyond that, something can be said about the story, about the author, or about the performance. Just don't give away the plot! After the introduction, the readers wait to begin until they're all in place and frozen and the audience is quiet.

At the end, the last words are spoken slowly and with rhythm, so the audience knows the story is over. Everyone recognizes the ending "*happily ever after.*" But the same effect can be achieved with almost any words by reading them in a "slow three."

When the story is finished, the readers freeze for a long moment to break the action. Then they close their scripts, face the audience, and bow all together.

Once young people have a general idea of how Readers Theatre works, they can take over much of the staging themselves. In fact, they often beat adults at developing mime. After all, pretending is part of their profession.

It worked! Readers Theatre in second grade

Sheri J. Forsythe

VOLUME 49, NUMBER 3, NOVEMBER 1995

"Second graders can write and present their own Readers Theatre."

This statement by my professor, Dr. James Flood, brought me up short. Not in my class, I thought; very few of the second graders entering my bilingual class in July are readers. But the challenge was there: Use Readers Theatre as a teaching tool. So I did. Now I'm glad I took the challenge. It worked!

Our school is on a year-round schedule so I plan in quarters using a thematic, integrated approach. I knew the students right out of first grade were not going to sit down and write a Readers Theatre for me, so I decided to work one step at a time.

In the first quarter of the year I introduced the concept of Readers Theatre using a Readers Theatre example from our language arts books. The whole class worked on the same project and each child was given the opportunity to choose the area s/he wanted to work in. A backdrop was drawn and painted, some props were made, and each student made a paper bag puppet. Cooperative groups practiced how to read and present a Readers Theatre. After much practice each group presented for the class, and then voted for the best presentation. This group became the main characters while the rest of the class took part in the chorus and nonspeaking parts. Since the class was still learning to use a microphone, I chose a fairly nonthreatening audience for the first presentation—the first-grade class taught by the teacher most of these students had the year before.

This first presentation, during the last week of the first quarter, was very successful and enjoyed by all. After vacation we started again. By this time my students' reading had improved substantially and I wanted everyone to have a speaking part.

I chose several different scripts I had written that were adaptations of books I used in the classroom. I again assigned groups, making sure that each group had students of varying reading levels. This time they used fewer props and concentrated more on reading, varying tone of voice, following the script, using the microphone, and being a good audience.

Everyone had a part; the nonreaders memorized theirs. When they were ready for the final production, each student wrote an invitation to her/his parents and we invited both first-grade classes and the other second-grade class to the production. This time the Readers Theatre was presented in the auditorium on a stage. Again, everyone did a great job. About a dozen parents attended and they were very pleased.

Next came the big step—writing. I decided a good place to start would be the adaptation of familiar stories that contained lots of dialogue. Using the overhead I modeled the process of changing from story form to Readers Theatre format. The students enjoyed following the story from the book and telling me who should be talking and what they should say. We identified what a narrator should say.

Next, we brainstormed some of our favorite books and stories. I listed everything the students suggested. Then the students chose, by vote, their five favorite stories.

At this point I determined how many parts each story should have. So that everyone had a chance to contemplate which Readers Theatre they wanted to work on, I reread each story several times to the class. Then, I let the students sign up for the story they wanted to work on— no teacher manipulation of groups, only size limitations. To my surprise and relief, the class formed five heterogeneous groups.

The next step was to write a script. I had a conference with each group to start them off and then monitored each group's progress. Additional conferences were necessary at least every other writing day. The students decided what should be said by each character and the narrators, and who in the group should play each part. In some groups a very low level reader wanted to read a long part. One group gave the low reader a main part and coached him; another group convinced the low reader that he was best suited for another part. There were no hurt feelings and all the students were pleased with what they were doing.

We had several class conferences to discuss how the project was progressing. There were a few complaints, which were resolved. And there was a pride in ownership. As each group finished writing, I typed the scripts on the computer, printed them, and made copies.

Then it was time to start practicing. Again we worked on reading with expression, following the script, using the microphone, and being a good audience. The groups scattered to read, then came together to practice in front of the whole class. Many students took their scripts home to study them. Again, the students wrote invitations to their families and we invited the primary classes. Over 20 parents came to our Readers Theatre presentation. The students and I were elated. Each group did a magnificent job.

Success had given me courage. Fourth quarter came and it was time for them to perform on their own. The unit of study at the time was the solar system. Since we had read several books about space, I gave a homework assignment to write a story about space that might make a good Readers Theatre script. I found some very good stories and received permission from several students to share their stories with the class. After a long discussion the class agreed upon 6 stories for the final Readers Theatre project.

We had open sign-ups for the project. One story was eliminated because no one signed up for it. Again, we had five heterogeneous groups ranging from four to eight students. We followed the same procedure as before, but the students found that creating a whole story was more difficult than just adapting another story. I have to admit that this was a lot of work, for teacher and students, but it was worth it. Some groups had to start over several times. Others had to adjust their scripts to the reading ability of less capable students or spend a lot of time tutoring. There was the last-minute rush to finish writing by our deadline.

After several scripts were printed, one group noticed that another group's script was longer than theirs; they wanted it back for revision to make it longer. On the last writing day five students gathered around my desk and dictated their script while I typed on my computer. The kids loved to watch their work appear on the computer screen. My only regret was that I did not have enough time and computers for the students to type their own scripts.

My school had planned a literature fair for the first week in June. We decided that Readers Theatre would be our entry for the fair and that the whole school and community would be our last audience. We videotaped our presentations and made a book of scripts. We actually taped

---

Readers Theatre stories

Here are a few books I found adaptable to Readers Theatre. There are many books and stories that can be easily adapted for use as Readers Theatres. The more dialogue the text contains the easier it is for the students to create a script. For longer books it is best to use just a brief excerpt or scene from the story.

Burningham, J. (1989). *Hey! Get off our train.* New York: Crown.
Carreno, M. (1987). *El viaje del joven Matsua.* Mexico City: Editorial Trillas.
Janosch. (1985). *El cocodrilo feliz.* Madrid: General Tabanera.
Scieszka, J. (1989). *The true story of the 3 little pigs!* New York: Viking Penguin.
Viorst, J. (1978). *Alexander who used to be rich last Sunday.* New York: Aladdin.
Viorst, J. (1982). *Alexander and the terrible, horrible, no good, very bad day.* New York: Aladdin.

---

each performance three times to get it just right! On the day of the literature fair the hallways were filled with beautiful projects and outside our door a crowd gathered all day to watch our video, which ran continuously. We never tired of watching the videos over and over again.

There are a few things that need to be clarified. The class had worked in cooperative groups starting in first grade and were very familiar with group dynamics. Each group always had a student facilitator (a leader), a scribe, an encourager, and a time keeper. We worked in cooperative groups across the curriculum.

There was an extreme range of abilities in the class. Several students worked with the resource specialist, but all participated in the Readers Theatre. Our classroom routine also included writers workshop and flexible reading groups, but the focus of the year was the Readers Theatre. Often the classroom was noisy and appeared to be in total chaos, but work was in progress. And, of course, all of our work was in Spanish.

Yes, it worked, Dr. Flood. My second graders wrote and performed their own Readers Theatre. At the end of the year all 30 students were comfortable standing before an audience and speaking into a microphone; in fact they loved it. All my students were successful. They were proud of their accomplishments, but not nearly as proud as I was.

Integrating music, reading, and writing at the primary level

Diane Langfitt

Volume 47, Number 5, February 1994

I am certain that you have heard catchy jingles that have rattled around in your brain for years or even decades. I'd even be willing to guess that you first learned the ABCs in a song, and it wasn't until later that you actually became acquainted with the letters of the alphabet visually, auditorily, and kinesthetically. Music is a powerful medium that educators can and should incorporate into their classrooms. I like to capitalize on the power of music to help primary students become successful readers and writers.

At the emergent and beginning reading levels, young children need many cues to help them make meaning from print. Along with the usual semantic, syntactic, graphophonic, or picture cues that we emphasize, a simple melody is another cue that is useful for young students. A familiar or simple melody included in book that students read and write assures success.

Generally, my music/reading/writing lessons center around the theme that is being emphasized in the classroom. For example, on a visit to a village school last February, I noticed that the room was decorated in a winter theme. I decided to capitalize on that theme and have the students create their own class book about what they like to do in the winter.

To begin the lesson, I read the book *My Favorite Time of Year* by Susan Pearson (1988). We then discussed the seasons and winter in particular. I suggested we write a class book about what we like to do in the winter. After one student offered that he "liked to sled on the hills," I suggested that we could use a melody in our book. I wrote the first line on the chalkboard and then sang it for the class to the tune of "She'll Be Comin' 'Round the Mountain."

> We'll be sliding on the hills at wintertime.
> We'll be sliding on the hills at wintertime.
> We'll be sliding on the hills, we'll be sliding on the hills,
> We'll be sliding on the hills at wintertime.

The students chimed in as soon as they recognized the tune, and soon everyone wanted to write a verse to our song. They included: "We'll be skating on the ice at wintertime," "We'll be drinking hot cocoa at wintertime," and "We'll be playing basketball at wintertime." In very little time we had 22 different verses in our book.

During recess I typed the words on the computer, printed out a verse on the bottom of each page, and later in the day the students illustrated their pages. We bound it with a cover and title page, complete with a city of publication and copyright date. In one hour of class time we had a beautiful class book (which the students wanted to copy for the library) that all of the students could read and sing.

While I wrote the verses on the chalkboard, I stressed various reading concepts. I asked students to help spell words by listening to the sounds, to look for patterns of words, and to look at the structure of words (e.g., there was an -ing word in each line).

This lesson can be adapted and changed to fit any theme using many common children's songs. In order to implement such a lesson, I first brainstorm songs that have a simple, patterned verse and then write new words that fit the theme. The following are some common tunes and suggestions for implementing them:

Tune: "The Farmer in the Dell"

Animal unit: The bear lives in a cave. The bear lives in a cave. We all have a place to live. The bear lives in a cave.

Tune: "The Farmer in the Dell"

Initial consonant sounds: Apple starts with A. Apple starts with A. Words are made of letters. Apple starts with A.

Tune: "A Hunting We Will Go"

Rhyming Words: A hunting we will go. A hunting we will go. We'll catch a puffin, feed him a muffin, and then we'll let him go.

Tune: "Mary Wore a Red Dress"

Nutrition: Betty ate some oranges, oranges, oranges. Betty ate some oranges, she got strong.

Tune: "She'll Be Comin' 'Round the Mountain"

Seasons, special times: We'll be eating lots of cookies at Christmastime.

Tune: "The Wheels on the Bus"

Transportation: The prop on the plane goes round and round.

Along with each music/reading/writing lesson, I also read aloud a piece of children's literature that goes with the theme. In some lessons, the literature is used as the jumping-off point from which we discuss and then write our own book. At other times, literature is used as a final activity to wrap up and confirm what we have just accomplished.

The pattern and melody of their new book, along with the illustrations, help the children to read their class book independently. I have seen hundreds of emergent and beginning readers pick up these class books and read them to others. If time permits, I also make smaller books for each individual to take home. The books have been a big hit with families that excitedly watch their children's enthusiasm for reading.

One of our most important jobs as teachers is to instill in children the love of reading. There is no better way to help young children feel excited about reading than to help them create and read their own books. Your students' pride and enthusiasm for their accomplishments will be a terrific reward.

REFERENCE

Pearson, S. (1988). *My favorite time of year.* New York: Scholastic.

Enhancing stories through the use of musical sound

Fred Kersten

Volume 49, Number 8, May 1996

Students in Mrs. Kistler's second grade at Wallaceton-Boggs Elementary School in Phillipsburg, Pennsylvania, were excited! Today they were going to hear the story *Snow White*. But something was different—there was a box of musical instruments in the front of the room. Their reader for today, Dr. Kersten, was passing out nametags for each of the characters identified in the story. He explained that they had to think about the person or animal they were to be and select an instrument to play when their character's name was spoken. Then they were to make up a rhythm or melody that they could play each time the character was mentioned as the story was read.

Each student thought critically and then selected an instrument. The Prince was portrayed by a pair of hand cymbals played forte (loud) and climactic. Snow White was represented by a tambourine—piano (soft) and jingly. When it was discovered that there were more characters than children in the room, the student teacher, her university adviser, and Mrs. Kistler assumed character roles. Also, several students represented two characters to complete the cast.

When they were ready, the story began. The students listened keenly, ready to play their instruments when their characters were mentioned. The reader paused slightly after mentioning each character so full appreciation could be made of each child's contribution. Uncertainty resulted when a generalization, "small animals," occurred, as students had been given specific identities such as birds and deer, but several students played at once, illustrating conceptual understanding. When the dwarfs returned home from work, the reader paused and switched on a prerecorded tape of "Hi-Ho" from the Walt Disney recording. Several students moved their hands to the music; they also could have sung the well-known melody.

Occasionally a student would hesitate, but attentive help from peers encouraged the unsure to play, making the enterprise a cooperative venture. As the class interacted with the spoken text, listening skills were honed, and appreciation of the story was highlighted as each character assumed a "now" identity, personified by a member of the class. In written letters I received from each student weeks later, the second graders still clearly identified themselves with the characters they personified, illustrating a continued recall of identity and the story plot.

A new idea? Not really, but an idea that can be put to good use by elementary classroom teachers and music specialists who would like to obtain new levels of creativity, attentiveness, and interest from students. While oral reading activities are important and are included in most elementary classes, they can be passive in terms of student involvement. After several readings of the same story, students can add luster and excitement to the action by interpreting it with sound. The main requirements for this activity are a quantity of sources (rhythm, Orff, or homemade instruments) and a desire by both teacher and class to experiment with musical sounds.

Getting started

Initially, an inventory should be made of available sound sources. Rhythm instruments should be considered first because of availability and ease of playing. the following instruments have proven valuable in the enhancement of stories and may be readily available in the music room or learning resource center, or individually available from colleagues:

- Hand drums (sometimes available from physical education instructors)

- Maracas
- Bell sprays (jingle bells on a strap or wrist band work just as well)
- Whip (can be made from two pieces of wood)
- Claves (sticks)
- Bongos
- Tambourines
- Cymbals (good ones can be borrowed from the band director)
- Cowbells
- Wood blocks
- Triangles

As a public school music teacher, I was fortunate to receive a donation of an old drum set. It provided quality sound sources, including the much needed bass, snare, tom-tom drums, and quality cymbals. (Many times these instruments are available, and parents are happy to provide them when asked—especially drums!) Nontraditional sound sources including venetian blind slapping, book slamming, tacks rattling in an empty paper clip box, and a homemade nail xylophone are also possibilities.

Once the sound sources have been identified, experimentation by the teacher and students should take place. Explore musical concepts! Are the sounds long, short, sharp, high, or low? Can you make them fast, slow, loud, or soft? Can you describe each sound in some way? What impressions do the students receive from each sound? Discuss the sounds as part of a science exploration unit emphasizing terms such as vibration, attack, decay, and duration. Explore metal, wood, and membrane sources as to the varying timbres and why they occur. Through this activity words such as *mellow, hollow, silvery, jangling*, and others can become part of each student's vocabulary.

The story

Most stories can be enhanced with sound sources immediately by the children. However, it is a good idea to have the first such undertaking guided by the teacher. Once students become aware of the process and possibilities, their own ideas will abound.

Identification of main story characters is a first step. For example, if one of the characters in the story is a king, regal sound sources can be substituted for his spoken name. The sound sources may serve as an accompaniment to the spoken word each time his name is mentioned. Actions can be realistically depicted by the sounds. Walking can be rhythmic in nature; fighting might include many of the louder instruments, and the sound duration may be increased.

If a story has many places where enhancements can be included, the teacher should develop a pictorial representation of characters and actions on a large sheet of paper. Using this aid, the instructor can point to the pictures when the sound is to be produced. A small diagram of the instrument or its name can be placed next to the character or action as an added aid.

Once the musical enhancement has been created the words of the story can be omitted as a variation, and a composition of representational nature will result. This sound piece presents many possibilities for interpretation by others as a creation with a plot without verbal expression.

Creating stories with musical sound

Sound sources present wonderful opportunities for literary creation by the class. Developing an original story, adding sound, writing it as prose or poetry, and recording it on cassette incorporates many of the tenets of whole language. Once the story is in written format, it may be illustrated and then bound as a book for the classroom library. As the story involves musical sounds, a cassette recording can be included with the copy enhancing its attractiveness.

Imagination should be allowed to run wild! For those students who find creative expression difficult during the initial stages of production, a broad title, such as "The Ghost Walks," will serve as an icebreaker for brainstorming. Another idea for original participation is a story composed about members of the class. Students' hobbies, pets, home activities, and play provide ample material for fashioning a title, plot, and text.

The role of the music specialist

As activities of this nature are initiated and sophisticated, a music specialist can do many things to aid in quality renditions. If xylophones, Orff instruments, or other barred instruments are used, certain chords or pentatonic scales may be illustrated as a way the instruments will sound best. Recommendations and demonstrations of ostinatos, rondo forms, and verse-refrain formats are another way *music*, not noise, may come to be created and produced. Illustrating how maracas are played or the way to hold and play a wood block or triangle can be regarded as part of the specialist's role. Observations of performances and nonauthoritarian suggestions by the music specialist can help each class render music as enhancement to the stories read.

Stories read in class can be enhanced through the use of musical sounds in a creative manner. The classroom teacher need not have an extensive background in music. Through the use of available sound sources, main characters and designated actions can be portrayed. Student ideas and participation should be actively solicited.

The enhancement process need not be complex. Detailed scoring and sophisticated resources are not a requirement. Any classroom teacher desiring to add life to stories previously read should try to enhance them with sound. Students and teachers will find the results far exceed the time and effort put forth in the development of this activity.

Read with a beat: Developing literacy through music and song

Gayla R. Kolb

Volume 50, Number 1, September 1996

Music is a language with powerful appeal. Children, especially, are captivated by the music in their environment. They respond freely to a variety of tempos, from drum beating to gentle swaying, and their undivided attention commits to memory verse after verse of popular songs and jingles. The enthusiasm displayed and the eagerness to sing and move with the beat reflect a child's natural propensity toward music.

The spontaneous disposition children have toward rhythm and melody makes music an ideal tool for assisting them with the interwoven facets of language: listening, speaking, reading, and writing. Through music, children experience the wholeness of language. The ideas and emotions communicated are presented in meaningful context, and the melody and lyrics provide a source for interacting with the thoughts of others. In addition, the emotive quality and the structure of musical composition engage children in fulfilling personal meanings (Harp, 1988).

> Music and reading go together because singing is a celebration of language. Children's language naturally has rhythm and melody. Children bring this natural "music" language with them to the task of learning to read, and so using singing to teach reading draws on this natural understanding. (Harp, 1988, p. 454)

A most effective way to teach children to learn and to value language is to provide them with a variety of meaningful experiences that fine-tune their ability to hear rhythm, sounds, and melodies. The skill children gain in listening will then provide a solid framework for successfully attending to language in print (Martin, Brogan, & Archambault, 1990). The singing-reading connection not only helps children learn to read but also fosters a love for reading (Handy, 1989).

Integrating music with reading—Getting started

A first step toward integrating songs into the reading curriculum is simply to sing a song repeatedly until children are comfortable with the tune and the lyrics (Barclay & Walwer, 1992; Handy, 1989; Harp, 1988; Renegar, 1990). Picture cards in a pocket chart or on a flannel board may be used to assist children with learning the lyrics (Handy, 1989). Creating motions to act out the song also helps children recall the words (Renegar, 1990). It is helpful to tape-record each song and provide children with a special area where they can listen to the tapes.

Next, the children are ready to see the lyrics in print. When using a song picture book, the teacher should introduce the book to children in the same manner as any picture book, with a discussion of the cover and illustrations, a complete reading of the book, and a sharing time at the end (Handy, 1989; Harp, 1988). Choral and echo reading techniques are also effective ways to help children connect the song to print.

Printing the lyrics on chart paper so that children can participate in a variety of reading experiences will also help promote print awareness. Activities such as pointing to each word as it is sung, locating words that appear in more than one place, and providing children with word cards to match like words are excellent ways to reinforce the link between speech and print (Harp, 1988; Renegar, 1990). The recreation of the song using sentence strips will help children to develop sequencing and to understand the relationship between sentences and the whole composition (Handy, 1989; Renegar, 1990).

After many opportunities to read the song in print, the children are now ready to participate in various activities designed to extend the singing-reading experience.

Book concepts

Shared book experiences. Introduce and read a variety of song picture books such as *Farmer in the Dell* and *Down by the Bay* using the shared-book approach (Holdaway, 1979). The initial reading should encourage prediction, promote some discussion, and be followed by later readings from a large chart on which the lyrics of the song have been written.

Book talks. Encourage children to share and discuss song picture books that are of interest. The discussion of rhymes, language patterns, illustrations, favorite parts, characters, and events can lead to grand conversations—all of which help children integrate their understanding of language and books.

Sight vocabulary

Word sorts. Print song lyrics on individual word cards and have students categorize them; then justify and title each category.

Word games. Play word games such as Concentration to help children learn song words by sight. Write the lyrics on pairs of word cards, turn them face down, and then have children take turns turning over and reading the cards until all cards have been matched.

Word banks. After children recognize and read song word cards consistently, deposit them into individual word banks. As each bank grows, sort the words into various word categories.

Reading comprehension

Cloze technique. Omit every 10th word or key words from songs. Have children read and fill in the missing parts. Identify context clues that help children decide upon their answers (Handy, 1989).

Story maps. Use story maps to help children identify and organize the elements of songs such as the song's characters, events, problem, solution, and main idea.

Music response journals. Provide children with individual music journals in which they can write their thoughts and feelings about songs and singing-reading activities (Davenport, 1990).

Fluency

Support reading/singing. Use choral and echo reading and singing activities to help children develop smooth reading.

Chants. Chant a variety of jingles and street rhymes to assist children with the development of phrasing and intonation. Other suggested activities include clapping to the beat, playing rhythm instruments, and choral chanting.

Music and song in an early reading program have great value. As noted, a wide variety of music and singing activities combined with reading instruction can foster beginning reading success. Specifically, they can facilitate the development of book concepts, sight vocabulary, reading comprehension, and fluency. It is most important to note that because children have a natural love for music and singing, music-integrated reading instruction can help foster a love for lifelong reading. So, the next time it is story time, remember, read with a beat!

REFERENCES

Barclay, D.K., & Walwer, L. (1992). Linking lyrics and literacy through song picture books. *Young Children, 47*(4), 76–85.

Davenport, M.R. (1990, March). *The magic of music: Literacy through song.* Paper presented at the annual meeting of the Missouri Council of the International Reading Association, Columbia, MO.

Handy, S. (1989). *The singing-reading connection.* Hilmar, CA: Troubadour Learning.

Harp, B. (1988). Why are your kids singing during reading time? *The Reading Teacher, 41,* 454–456.

Holdaway, D. (1979). *The foundations of literacy.* New York: Ashton Scholastic.

Martin, B., Brogan, P., & Archambault, J. (1990). *Sounds of a powwow.* Allen, TX: DLM.

Renegar, L.S. (1990). Using predictable songs in beginning reading activities. *Reading Horizons, 31*(1), 35–38.

Music and children's books

Kathleen Jacobi-Karna

VOLUME 49, NUMBER 3, NOVEMBER 1995

Do you "see a song" when you read children's books? Eric Carle extends this invitation in the opening paragraph of his otherwise wordless book, *I See A Song*. Students see a song in Bill Martin's *Brown Bear, Brown Bear, What Do You See?* because of its sing-song text that involves them from the very first hearing. Students seeing the song *I Know an Old Lady Who Swallowed a Fly* are quick to note variations among the illustrated versions. There are many books available that can bring music into classrooms to help students see a song.

In the ongoing discussion about curriculum integration, teachers search for ways to connect music, art, language, math, reading, and writing. Such integration is indeed more interesting for students and of greater importance, more connected to their lives outside of school. Children read, write, draw, and sing as they interact with their world. In the remainder of this article, I briefly discuss categories of children's literature that help integrate music into the classroom.

Illustrated songs are a popular combination of music and books. Songs offer students opportunities to sing in class, explore uses of language, and create new lyrics. Comparing different versions of the same song encourages students to create their own.

Music plays various roles in fictional books. Through stories, students learn about careers in music, musical instruments, and famous compositions. Books such as these expose students to people involved in music and tell how music affects their lives. They also provide an occasion for students to become acquainted with some well known musical compositions.

Books that have repetitive and/or additive texts enable the teacher to reinforce the concepts of sequence, refrain, and timbre (tone color). Students can chant recurring refrains, add sound effects with instruments, and even dramatize these stories.

There is a close relationship between rhythmic texts and music. Concepts such as steady beat and rhythm are a common focus when working with books of poems, rhymes, and chants. Assigning small groups to read each voice provides students with an "ensemble" experience that encourages cooperation.

Wordless books offer opportunities for students to accompany the illustra-

Children's books with musical possibilities

Illustrated songs

Adams, P. (1993). *There was an old lady who swallowed a fly*. Singapore: Child's Play.

Aliki. (1968). *Hush little baby: A folk lullaby*. New York: Little Simon.

Bangs, E. (1976). *Steven Kellogg's Yankee Doodle*. New York: Parent's Magazine Press.

Baum, S. (1992). *Today is Monday*. New York: HarperCollins.

Bonne, R. (1961). *I know an old lady*. Ill. A. Graboff. New York: Scholastic.

Brett, J. (1989). *The twelve days of Christmas*. New York: G.P. Putnam's Sons.

Carle, E. (1993). *Today is Monday*. New York: Philomel.

Chamberlain, S. (1991). *The friendly beasts: A traditional Christmas carol*. New York: Dutton.

Child, L.M. (1989). *Over the river and through the wood*. Ill. I. Van Rynbach. Boston: Little, Brown.

Child, L.M. (1993). *Over the river and through the wood*. Ill. C. Manson. New York: North-South.

Emberley, E. (1967). *London Bridge is falling down*. Boston: Little, Brown.

Fernandes, E. (1993). *Waves in the bathtub*. Richmond Hill, Ontario: North Winds.

Galdone, P. (1985). *Cat goes fiddle-i-fee*. New York: Clarion.

Gries, J. (1992). *Where the buffalo roam*. Nashville: Ideals Children's Books.

Hale, S.J. (1984). *Mary had a little lamb*. Ill. T. dePaola. New York: Holiday House.

Hale, S.J. (1990). *Mary had a little lamb*. Ill. B. McMillan. New York: Scholastic.

Hawkins, C., & Hawkins, J. (1987). *I know an old lady who swallowed a fly*. New York: G.P. Putnam's Sons.

Hurd, T. (1984). *Mama don't allow*. New York: Harper & Row.

Ivimey, J.W. (1987). *The complete story of the three blind mice*. Ill. P. Galdone. New York: Clarion.

Jeffers, S. (1984). *Silent night*. New York: E.P. Dutton.

Johnson, J.W., & Johnson J.R. (1970). *Lift every voice and sing: Words and music*. Ill. M. Thompson. New York: Hawthorne.

Keats, E.J. (1968). *The little drummer boy*. New York: Macmillan.

Knight, H. (1981). *The twelve days of Christmas*. New York: Macmillan.

Kovalski, M. (1987). *The wheels on the bus*. Boston: Joy Street.

Kovalski, M. (1988). *Jingle bells*. Boston: Joy Street.

Langstaff, J. (1977). *Oh, a-hunting we will go*. Ill. N. Winslow Parker. New York: Atheneum.

Manson, C. (1992). *A farmyard song: An old rhyme with new pictures*. New York: North-South.

Manson, C. (1993). *The tree in the wood*. New York: North-South.

McCarthy, B. (1987). *Buffalo girls*. New York: Crown.

Oberhansli, T. (1967). *Sleep, baby, sleep*. New York: Atheneum.

Pearson, T.C. (1983). *We wish you a merry Christmas: A traditional Christmas carol*. New York: E.P. Dutton.

Peek, M. (1985). *Mary wore her red dress and Henry wore his green sneakers*. New York: Clarion.

Pienkowski, J. (1989). *Oh my a fly!* Los Angeles: Price Stern Sloan. *(continued)*

Quackenbush, R. (1974). *There'll be a hot time in the old town tonight.* Philadelphia: J.P. Lippincott.

Raffi. (1987). *Shake my sillies out.* Ill. D. Allender. New York: Crown.

Raffi. (1990). *Wheels on the bus.* Ill. S.K. Wickstrom. New York: Crown.

Raffi. (1992). *Baby beluga.* Ill. A. Wolff. New York: Crown.

Roffey, M., & Lodge, B. (1993). *The grand old Duke of York.* New York: Whispering Coyote.

Rounds, G. (1990). *I know an old lady who swallowed a fly.* New York: Holiday House.

Seeger, P., & Seeger, C. (1973). *The foolish frog.* Ill. M. Jagr. New York: Macmillan.

Shoemaker, K. (1980). *Children go where I send thee.* Minneapolis, MN: Winston.

Simon, P. (1991). *At the zoo.* Ill. V. Michaut. New York: Doubleday.

Spier, P. (1961). *The fox went out on a chilly night.* New York: Doubleday.

Spier, P. (1970). *The Erie Canal.* Garden City, NY: Doubleday.

Spier, P. (1973). *The star-spangled banner.* Garden City, NY: Doubleday.

Staines, B. (1989). *All God's critters got a place in the choir.* Ill. M. Zemach. New York: E.P. Dutton.

Stanley, D. (1979). *Fiddle-i-fee: A traditional American chant.* Boston: Little, Brown.

Steven, J. (1981). *Animal fair.* New York: Holiday House.

Sweet, M. (1992). *Fiddle-i-fee: A farmyard song for the very young.* Boston: Little, Brown.

Taylor, J. (1992). *Twinkle, twinkle, little star.* Ill. J. Noonan. New York: Scholastic.

Trapani, I. (1993). *The itsy bitsy spider.* New York: Whispering Coyote.

Wallner, J. (1990). *Good King Wenceslas.* New York: Philomel.

Watson, W. (1990). *Frog went a-courting.* New York: Lothrop, Lee and Shepard.

Westcott, N.B. (1989). *Skip to my Lou.* Boston: Little, Brown.

Wildsmith, B. (1972). *The twelve days of Christmas.* New York: Franklin Watts.

Zelinsky, P.O. (1990). *The wheels on the bus.* New York: Dutton.

Zemach, H. (1966). *Mommy, buy me a china doll.* Ill. M. Zemach. Chicago: Follett.

Zemach, M. (1976). *Hush, little baby.* New York: E. P. Dutton.

Zuromski, D. (1978). *The farmer in the dell.* Boston: Little, Brown.

Fiction

Ackerman, K. (1988). *Song and dance man.* Ill. S. Gammell. New York: Knopf.

Ambrus, V. (1978). *Mishka.* New York: Frederick Warne.

Baylor, B. (1982). *Moon song.* Ill. R. Himler. New York: Charles Scribner's Sons.

Botsford, W. (1981). *The pirates of Penzance.* Ill. E. Sorel. New York: Random House.

Brett, J. (1991). *Berlioz the bear.* New York: G. P. Putnam's Sons.

Brott, A. (1990). *Jeremy's decision.* Ill. M. Martchenko. Brooklyn, NY: Kane/Miller.

Carlstrom, N.W. (1993). *What does the rain play?* Ill. H. Sorenson. New York: Macmillan.

Carey, V.S. (1990). *Quail song.* Ill. I. Barnett. New York: Whitebird.

Catalano, D. (1992). *Wolf plays alone.* New York: Philomel.

Clement, C. (1988). *The voice of the wood.* Ill. F. Clement. New York: Dial.

Clement, C. (1989). *Musician from the darkness.* Ill. J. Howe. Boston: Little, Brown.

Ernst, L.C. (1989). *When bluebell sang.* New York: Bradbury.

Fleischman, P. (1988). *Rondo in C.* Ill. J. Wentworth. New York: Harper & Row.

Goble, P. (1992). *Love flute.* New York: Bradbury.

(continued)

Griffith, H.V. (1986). *Georgia music.* Ill. J. Stevenson. New York: Greenwillow.

Haseley, D. (1983). *The old banjo.* Ill. S. Gammell. New York: Macmillan.

Hirschi, R. (1991). *Harvest song.* Ill. D. Haeffele. New York: Cobblehill.

Hoffman, E.T.A. (1990). *The nutcracker.* Retold. J. Richardson. Ill. F. Crespi. New York: Arcade.

Hogrogian, N. (1988). *The cat who loved to sing.* New York: Knopf.

Hoopes, L.L. (1990). *Wing-a-ding.* Ill. S. Gammell. Boston: Little, Brown.

Isadora, R. (1979). *Ben's trumpet.* New York: Scholastic.

Johnston, T. (1987). *Whale song.* Ill. E. Young. New York: G.P. Putnam's Sons.

Johnston, T. (1988). *Pages of music.* Ill. T. dePaola. New York: G.P. Putnam's Sons.

Johnston, T. (1991). *Grandpa's song.* Ill. B. Sneed. New York: Dial.

Keats, E.J. (1971). *Apt. 3.* New York: Macmillan.

Keats, E.J. (1977). *Whistle for Willie.* New York: Penguin.

Kherdian, D., & Hogrogian, N. (1990). *The cat's midsummer jamboree.* New York: Philomel.

Kraus, R. (1990). *Musical Max.* Ill. J. Arrugo & A. Dewey. New York: Simon & Schuster.

Kuskin, K. (1982). *The philharmonic gets dressed.* Ill. M. Simont. New York: Harper & Row.

Lasker, D. (1979). *The boy who loved music.* Ill. J. Lasker. New York: Viking.

Lemieux, M. (1991). *Peter and the wolf.* New York: Morrow.

Lewis, R. (1991). *All of you was singing.* Ill. E. Young. New York: Atheneum.

Lobel, A. (1966). *The troll music.* New York: Harper & Row.

London, J. (1993). *Hip cat.* Ill. W. Hubbard. San Francisco, CA: Chronicle.

Luenn, N. (1993). *Song for the ancient forest.* Ill. J. Kastner. New York: Atheneum.

Mahy, M. (1990). *The pumpkin man and the crafty creeper.* Ill. H. Craig. New York: Lothrop, Lee & Shepard.

Martin, B., Jr, & Archambault, J. (1986). *Barn dance!* Ill. T. Rand. New York: Henry Holt.

Melmed, L.K. (1993). *The first song ever sung.* Ill. E. Young. New York: Lothrop, Lee & Shepard.

Micucci, C. (1989). *A little night music.* New York: Morrow.

Miranda, A. (1993). *Night songs.* New York: Bradbury.

Price, L. (1990). *Aida.* Ill. L. Dillon & D. Dillon. San Diego, CA: Gulliver.

Prokofiev, S. (1985). *Peter and the wolf.* Ill. B. Cooney. New York: Viking Penguin.

Root, P. (1986). *Soup for supper.* Ill. S. Truesdell. New York: Harper & Row.

Rylant, C. (1988). *All I see.* Ill. P. Catalanotto. New York: Orchard.

Schroeder, A. (1989). *Ragtime Tumpie.* Ill. B. Fuchs. Boston: Little, Brown.

Seeger, P. (1986). *Abiyoyo.* Ill. M. Hayes. New York: Scholastic.

Sheldon, D. (1991). *The whale's song.* Ill. G. Blythe. New York: Dial.

Vaughan, M. K. (1984). *Wombat stew.* Ill. P. Lofts. Morristown, NJ: Silver Burdett.

Volker, J.A. (1991). *Song of the chirimia.* Minneapolis, MN: Carolrhoda.

Williams, V.B. (1983). *Something special for me.* New York: Mulberry.

Williams, V.B. (1984). *Music, music for everyone.* New York: Greenwillow.

Wilson, S. (1991). *Garage song.* Ill. B. Karlin. New York: Simon & Schuster.

Winter, J. (1988). *Follow the drinking gourd.* New York: Knopf.

(continued)

Yeoman, J. (1990). *Old Mother Hubbard's dog learns to play*. Ill. Q. Blake. Boston: Houghton Mifflin.

Zolotow, C. (1982). *The song*. Ill. N. Tafuri. New York: Greenwillow.

Repetitive

Aylesworth, J. (1991). *Country crossing*. Ill. T. Rand. New York: Atheneum.

Baer, G. (1989). *Thump, thump, rat-a-tat-tat*. Ill. L. Ehlert. New York: Harper Trophy.

Carlstrom, N.W. (1992). *Baby-o*. Ill. S. Stevenson. Boston: Little, Brown.

Ericson, J.A. (1993). *No milk!* Ill. O. Eitan. New York: Tambourine.

Guthrie, D. (1990). *The witch has an itch*. Ill. K. Keck Arnsteen. New York: Little Simon.

Herson, K.D. (1989). *The copycat*. Ill. C. Stock. New York: Atheneum.

Kalan, R. (1981). *Jump, frog, jump!* Ill. B. Barton. New York: Mulberry.

Kesselman, W. (1982). *There's a train going by my window*. Ill. T. Chen. New York: Doubleday.

Van Laan, N. (1990). *Possum come a-knockin'*. Ill. G. Booth. New York: Knopf.

Viorst, J. (1972). *Alexander and the terrible, horrible, no good, very bad day*. Ill. R. Cruz. New York: Macmillan.

Ziefert, H. (1990). *Parade*. Ill. S. Mandel. New York: Bantam Little Rooster.

Additive

Aardema, V. (1981). *Bringing the rain to Kapiti Plain*. Ill. B. Vidal. New York: Dial.

Emberly, B. (1967). *Drummer Hoff*. Ill. E. Emberly. New York: Prentice Hall.

Galdone, P. (1961). *The house that Jack built*. New York: McGraw-Hill.

Galdone, P. (1975). *The gingerbread boy*. New York: Clarion.

Hayes, S. (1990). *The grumpalump*. Ill. B. Firth. New York: Clarion.

Kent, J. (1971). *The fat cat: A Danish folktale*. New York: Parent's Magazine.

Martin, B., Jr. (1993). *Old devil wind*. Ill. B. Root. San Diego, CA: Harcourt Brace.

McGovern, A. (1967). *Too much noise*. Ill. S. Taback. Boston: Houghton Mifflin.

Morgan, P. (1990). *The turnip: An old Russian folktale*. New York: Philomel.

Stow, J. (1992). *The house that Jack built*. New York: Dial.

Stutson, C. (1993). *By the light of the Halloween moon*. Ill. K. Hawkes. New York: Lothrop, Lee & Shepard.

Williams, L. (1986). *The little old lady who was not afraid of anything*. Ill. M. Lloyd. New York: Thomas Y. Crowell.

Wood, A. (1984). *The napping house*. Ill. D. Wood. San Diego, CA: Harcourt Brace.

Poems, rhymes, and chants

Aylesworth, J. (1990). *The completed hickory dickory dock*. Ill. E. Christelow. New York: Atheneum.

Barnes-Murphey, R. (1987). *One, two buckle my shoe: A book of counting rhymes*. New York: Little Simon.

Bayer, J. (1984). *A my name is Alice*. Ill. S. Kellogg. New York: E.P. Dutton.

Brown, M. (1980). *Finger rhymes*. New York: E.P. Dutton.

Brown, M. (1985). *Hand rhymes*. New York: E.P. Dutton.

(continued)

Brown, R. (1988). *Ladybug, ladybug*. New York: E.P. Dutton.

Carle, E. (1989). *Animals, animals*. New York: Philomel.

Carle, E. (1991). *Dragons, dragons, and other creatures that never were*. Comp. L. Whipple. New York: Philomel.

deRegniers, B.S. (Ed.). (1988). *Sing a song of popcorn: Every child's book of poems*. New York: Scholastic.

Gill, S. (1987). *The Alaska Mother Goose*. Ill. S. Cartwright. Homer, AK: Paws IV.

Fleischman, P. (1985). *I am phoenix*. New York: Harper & Row.

Fleischman, P. (1988). *Joyful noise: Poems for two voices*. New York: Harper & Row.

Higginson, W.J. (1991). *A collection of haiku*. Ill. S. Speidel. New York: Simon & Schuster.

Jorgenson, G. (1988). *Crocodile beat*. Il. P. Mullens. New York: Bradbury.

Joseph, L. (1990). *Coconut kind of day*. Ill. S. Speidel. New York: Puffin.

Keats, E.J. (1971). *Over in the meadow*. New York: Four Winds.

Kessler, L. (1980). *Hey diddle diddle*. Champaign, IL: Garrard.

Kessler, L. (1980). *Hickory dickory dock*. Ill. D. Cushman. Champaign, IL: Garrard.

Lenski, L. (1987). *Sing a song of people*. Ill. G. Laroche. Boston: Little, Brown.

Livingston, M.C. (1984). *Sky songs*. Ill. L.E. Fisher. New York: Holiday House.

Livingston, M.C. (1986). *Earth songs*. Ill. L.E. Fisher. New York: Holiday House.

Livingston, M.C. (1988). *Space songs*. Ill. L.E. Fisher. New York: Holiday House.

Lotz, K.E. (1993). *Snowsong whistling*. Ill. W. Kleven. New York: E.P. Dutton.

Martin, B., Jr. (1983). *Brown bear, brown bear, what do you see?* Ill. E. Carle. New York: Holt, Rinehart, & Winston.

Martin, B., Jr. (1991). *Polar bear, polar bear, what do you hear?* Ill. E. Carle. New York: Henry Holt.

Martin, B., Jr, & Archambault, J. (1987). *Here are my hands*. Ill. T. Rand. New York: Henry Holt.

Martin, B., Jr, & Archambault, J. (1988). *Listen to the rain*. Ill. J. Endicott. New York: Henry Holt.

Martin, B., Jr, & Archambault, J. (1989). *Chicka chicka boom boom*. Ill. L. Ehlert. New York: Simon & Schuster.

Merriam, E. (1987). *Halloween ABC*. Ill. L. Smith. New York: Macmillan.

Prelutsky, J. (1984). *The new kid on the block*. Ill. J. Stevenson. New York: Greenwillow.

Prelutsky, J. (1986). *Ride a purple pelican*. Ill. G. Williams. New York: Greenwillow.

Prelutsky, J. (1991). *For laughing out loud: Poems to tickle your funny bone*. Ill. M. Priceman. New York: Knopf.

Rosen, M. (1989). *We're going on a bear hunt*. Ill. H. Oxenburg. New York: Margaret K. McElderry.

Sky-Peck, K. (Ed.). (1991). *Who has seen the wind? An illustrated collection of poetry for young people*. Museum of Fine Arts, Boston. New York: Rizzoli.

Sneve, V.D.H. (1989). *Dancing teepees: Poems of American Indian youth*. Ill. S. Gammell. New York: Holiday House.

Whitman, W. (1991). *I hear America singing*. Ill. R. Sabuda. New York: Philomel.

Wood, A. (1992). *Silly Sally*. San Diego, CA: Harcourt Brace.
(continued)

Wyndham, R. (Ed.). (1968). *Chinese Mother Goose rhymes*. Ill. E. Young. New York: Philomel.

Yolen, J. (Ed.). (1992). *Street rhymes around the world*. Honesdale, PA: Wordsong.

Wordless/limited text

Briggs, R. (1978). *The snowman*. New York: Random House.

Carle, E. (1973). *I see a song*. New York: Crowell.

Crews, D. (1982). *Carousel*. New York: Greenwillow.

dePaola, T. (1983). *Sing, Pierrot, sing: A picture book in mime*. San Diego, CA: Harcourt Brace.

Fuchs, E. (1969). *Journey to the moon*. New York: Delacorte.

Shulevitz, U. (1978). *Dawn*. New York: Farrar, Straus & Giroux.

Spier, P. (1986). *Dreams*. Garden City, NY: Doubleday.

Wildsmith, B. (1986). *Birds*. Oxford: Oxford University Press.

Wildsmith, B. (1989). *Fishes*. Oxford: Oxford University Press.

Wildsmith, B. (1991). *The circus*. Oxford: Oxford University Press.

Factual

Ardley, N. (1989). *Eyewitness books: Music*. New York: Knopf.

Botermans, J., Dewit, H., & Goddefroy, H. (1989). *Making and playing musical instruments*. Seattle, WA: University of Washington Press.

Cline, D. (1976). *Cornstalk fiddle and other homemade instruments*. New York: Oak Publications.

deSouza, C. (1989). *Exploring the arts: Listening to music*. London: Marshall Cavendish.

Fichter, G.S. (1978). *American Indian music and musical instruments*. New York: David McKay.

Haskins, J. (1992). *Amazing grace: The story behind the song*. Brookfield, CT: Millbrook.

Hughes, L. (1976). *The first book of jazz*. New York: Franklin Watts.

Kaner, E. (1991). *Sound science*. Ill. L. Phillips. New York: Addison-Wesley.

Krementz, J. (1991). *A very young musician*. New York: Simon & Schuster.

Nichols, J. (1992). *Women music makers: An introduction to women composers*. New York: Walker.

Paxton, A.K. (1986). *Making music*. New York: Atheneum.

Roalf, P. (1993). *Looking at paintings: Musicians*. New York: Hyperion.

Schaaf, P. (1980). *The violin close up*. New York: Four Winds.

Scheader, C. (1985). *Contributions of women: Music*. Minneapolis, MN: Dillon.

Sommer, E. (1992). *The kid's world almanac of music: From rock to Bach*. Ill. J. Lane. New York: World Almanac.

Ventura, P. (1988). *Great composers*. New York: G.P. Putnam's Sons.

Weil, L. (1991). *Wolferl: The first years in the life of Wolfgang Amadeus Mozart, 1756–1762*. New York: Holiday House.

tions with music. Students may use previously composed pieces or create their own sounds by improvising on instruments as they view the illustrations.

Factual books explore music in a variety of ways. Students can learn about the lives of famous composers or about how to construct their own musical instruments.

There are many books with "musical possibilities." The bibliography includes numerous titles in each of these categories. Accept Eric Carle's invitation, imagine, and "see a song."

Information about <u>Reading Online</u>, an online journal of the International Reading Association

In May 1997, the International Reading Association introduced a peer-reviewed professional journal available only on the Internet. Since then, *Reading Online* (www.readingonline.org) has become a leader in providing literacy resources and information. As a service to the worldwide community of educators, the Association makes the journal freely available to all those with Internet access.

Reading Online focuses on classroom literacy practice and research for educators working with students ages 5 to 18. A special mission of the journal is to support professionals as they explore new literacies and the integration of technology in the classroom, preparing students for a future in which literacy's meaning will continue to evolve and expand. Toward this goal, *ROL* invites readers to enter the journal, to read its text, watch its video, view its graphics, listen to its audio—and to shape its contents through participation and interaction.

The departments in *Reading Online* include the following:

Featured Articles

New ideas, action research, literacy theory, classroom suggestions, descriptions of practice—all this is available in peer-reviewed articles and invited commentaries at www.readingonline.org. Readers will find innovative pieces about using technology in the classroom and be challenged to think about new literacies in new ways. There also is information and ideas about "traditional" literacy and time-tested approaches and strategies readers can use in the classroom.

The Electronic Classroom

This department offers ideas about effective practice and new developments related to using technology in literacy teaching and learning. Full-length columns, Web watches and project descriptions, and regular contributions from leaders in the field explore current and developing technologies and their potential for the classroom. Readers are invited into the discussion to react to columns and features, and to share ideas and practices.

International Perspectives

Here *Reading Online* offers a forum for communication of ideas, literature, initiatives, and issues across nations and cultures. An international Web watch highlights Internet resources based around the globe. A regular column shares the magic of language and provides insights into a range of cultures through information about children's books. An international scholars section features the work of literacy leaders worldwide, and a notice board gives information about conferences where professionals can meet and exchange ideas.

New Literacies

This department presents a range of interpretations about reading, writing, and communicating—and encourages exploration and discussion of those interpretations and the meaning of literacy in our post-typographic age. In addition to featured columns on topics including critical literacy, media and multimedia literacy, and visual literacy, the department highlights innovative classroom work and offers a Web watch where readers can find descriptions of and links to other Internet resources.

Most important in *Reading Online* are the opportunities available for participation, communication, and professional dialogue. Online discussion forums on focused topics invite readers to share ideas and experiences, to ask questions and express concerns with colleagues around the world. Active links to e-mail addresses make it easy to send messages directly to authors, responding to their work or asking questions about it. *Reading Online* offers readers a whole new way of reading a professional journal.